FabJob® Guide to

BECOME A PERSONAL SHOPPER

BY LAURA HARRISON McBRIDE
PETER J. GALLANIS AND TAG GOULET

FABJOB® GUIDE TO
BECOME A PERSONAL SHOPPER
by Laura Harrison McBride, Peter J. Gallanis and Tag Goulet

ISBN 1-894638-55-7

National Library of Canada Cataloguing in Publication Data

McBride, Laura Harrison
    FabJob guide to become a personal shopper/
Laura Harrison McBride, Peter J. Gallanis and Tag Goulet.

Accompanied by a CD-ROM.
Includes bibliographical references.
ISBN 1-894638-55-7

1. Personal shoppers—Vocational guidance.
I. Goulet, Therese   II. Gallanis, Peter J.   III. Title.
TX335.M29 2005   640'.73   C2005-906446-8

FabJob Inc.
19 Horizon View Court
Calgary, Alberta, Canada T3Z 3M5

FabJob Inc.
4603 NE University Village #224
Seattle, Washington, USA 98105

To order books in bulk phone 403-949-2039
For media inquiries phone 403-949-4980

www.FabJob.com

About the Authors

The *FabJob Guide to Become a Personal Shopper* was written by Laura Harrison McBride, Peter J. Gallanis and Tag Goulet, with additional material by editor Jennifer James.

Laura Harrison McBride has shopped wildly on two continents. She once wore a floor-length, hooded mohair war cloak home from Ireland into the heat of a New York City July because it was too bulky to pack; she purchased the last bottle of 21-year-old Jameson's Irish Whiskey for a client, only to see it snatched at the airport. (She located one more last bottle in the US, however.) She has written numerous how-to books, including *How to Start a Gift Basket Business* for Simon & Schuster, as well as shopping articles for daily newspapers on topics such as how NOT to shop, and looking great all day, on any budget.

Peter J. Gallanis is a 10-year veteran of journalism and is currently managing editor of a trade magazine in Chicago, IL. He has worked formerly as a freelancer (Gallanis Freelance Writing Solutions) where his clients included the *Chicago Tribune*, and as an associate editor with *DSN Retailing Today*, a retail industry and fashion trade magazine. He began his career as a reporter, editor and columnist with two award-winning newspapers in Chicago's west suburbs. A 1993 graduate of Northern Illinois University where he earned a BA in English, he lives in Des Plaines, IL with his lovely wife Chriselda, son Alexander and daughter Antonia.

Tag Goulet is co-CEO of FabJob Inc. The company's website, FabJob.com, is visited by more than 50 million people per year and has been featured in many media including ABC, *Woman's Day*, Oprah.com, *Female Entrepreneur*, and stories at the *Wall Street Journal* and *Entrepreneur Magazine* websites. Tag has written and contributed to more than a dozen books, including a *USA Today* bestseller. Known as the "Breaking In" experts, Tag and her sister Catherine write a bi-weekly career column which is syndicated to newspapers in the U.S., Canada, and Europe, and their articles are published at leading career websites including MSN Careers and AOL.com. They are authors of the forthcoming book *Dream Careers*.

Contents

1. Introduction

As a personal shopper you will have a career that other people envy – getting paid to shop.

Shopping is North America's number-one hobby. When people aren't at work or home, their favorite place to be is the shopping mall. When they go on vacation, their preferred activity is shopping – even visitors to Las Vegas prefer shopping to gambling!

Many of us grew up with a love of shopping. A survey by Kurt Salmon Associates, a leading consulting firm to the retail industry, found that 88 percent of girls age 13 to 17 say they love shopping. We hear adults say they are "born to shop," "shop 'til you drop," and "when the going gets tough, the tough go shopping."

So if people love to shop so much, why do they need to hire personal shoppers? Because by the time most of us reach adulthood, we no longer have time to do everything we want to do. A March 2005 study by the Families and Work Institute reported that one in three American employees are chronically overworked, while 54 percent have felt over-whelmed at some time in the past month by how much work they have to complete.

People have less time for leisure, including shopping for clothing, gifts or even food. With the growing demands on their time, busy people are increasingly turning to personal shoppers. As a result, there are more opportunities than ever before to turn your love of shopping into a career.

You will discover how to get started and succeed in this fabulous career in this guide, the *FabJob Guide to Become a Personal Shopper*. This chapter lays the foundation for the rest of the guide. In the pages that follow, you will learn about the profession of personal shopping, different job titles that are commonly used, the many benefits of the career, and the steps to getting started.

1.1 Personal Shopping as a Profession

1.1.1 What Personal Shoppers Buy

A personal shopper is, simply, someone hired to shop for other people. While some personal shoppers specialize in a particular area, others may shop for virtually any product or service their clients want.

Many clients use personal shoppers when they spend the most money, typically during the winter holidays. According to 2004 data from the National Retail Federation, the top holiday gift desires among those surveyed (in order of most desired) were:

- Books, CDs, videos, video games

- Clothing and accessories

- Gift cards

- Consumer electronics

- Jewelry

- Home décor

As a personal shopper you could be hired to shop for any of these products – or any others that someone wants to give as Christmas or holiday gifts. However, while the December holiday season is a particularly busy time for personal shoppers, people need to buy things all year long.

One of the most popular specializations for personal shoppers is women's fashion. Personal shoppers are hired by all types of people from busy executives to working moms to help them look fabulous. Here is how *New York Magazine* described the work of personal shoppers in a 2001 "Best of New York" feature:

> *"...it's time to hit the stores, where they pick out things you would never see, like a Prada-esque suit on sale for $150, or a top that, combined with your old black pants, will make a very current, chic little outfit."*

These days, few people have the time they need to research markets, both brick and online, that offer an incredible number of things to choose from as corporate gifts or personal purchases. Add to that the fact that many people do not trust their own taste, and you have a ready-made population of potential clients ready for your help.

But personal shoppers are not only hired by individuals. A very lucrative specialty for some personal shoppers is buying gifts for corporate clients to give to their customers or employees.

Do you remember the famous shopping scene in the movie *Pretty Woman*? Julia Roberts' character needed a formal evening outfit for her date with Richard Gere's character. She went into a Beverly Hills boutique in her "working girl" clothes (too-short skirt, too-shiny boots, too-skimpy top, too-big hair) and almost got handed over to the police. It turned out all right in the end, but she certainly could have used the advice and assistance of a personal shopper.

If you work as a personal shopper for a retailer, most of your clients are likely to be wealthy and professional, but a few of your clients may need as much help as Julia Roberts' character. Just imagine how fun and rewarding it would be to help them look fabulous.

1.1.2 Who They Work For

Shopping careers offer two main options, both of which are covered in this guide: running your own business catering to various people or businesses; and working for a single large retailer or specialty boutique.

Working for Your Own Clients

Starting your own personal shopping business gives you the freedom and challenge of working with a variety of clients. In addition to clients who are too busy to shop for themselves, personal shoppers are also hired by people who are overwhelmed with the selection when it comes to making purchases, and want an expert to do their shopping for them. You may also work for clients who are physically unable to shop, and tourists unfamiliar with the shopping options available.

Depending on what each client needs, you may be hired to buy a whole wardrobe, or a single special item. Here are some possibilities:

- Being hired by busy executives to buy their gifts for the holidays

- Taking care of shopping for senior citizens and others who find it difficult to get around

- Shopping for high-end clothing, furniture, food, and other items for wealthy families

- Finding the perfect gift baskets or promotional items for a company to give to its important clients

- Purchasing all the new appliances and home furnishings for a client's newly built home, from storage to stereos

You will consult with clients about what they need and how much they want to spend, then you will make recommendations, find stores and companies that supply what your clients want, do the shopping and, if necessary, arrange for gift-wrapping or shipping. For your regular clients, you will keep track of their preferences and sizes, and remind them of special occasions when they will need gifts.

Chapter 3 has more information about the various tasks involved in personal shopping.

Working for a Company

If you prefer the security that comes with being an employee, consider working as a personal shopper for a company.

The retail industry is far ahead of any other industry in terms of sheer numbers of jobs for personal shoppers who want a steady paycheck. Most of these positions are with upscale stores. Among the many retailers that employ personal shoppers are: Bloomingdale's, Holt Renfrew, Macy's, Neiman Marcus, Nordstrom, Saks Fifth Avenue, and Tiffany & Co. There are also many boutiques and other retailers throughout North America that offer personal shopping services to their customers.

Susan Olden, vice president and director of Fifth Avenue Clubs for Saks Fifth Avenue, and a 34-year veteran in the retail business, concurs. While Saks doesn't release exact numbers, we do employ personal shoppers in 46 of our stores and there are lots of jobs out there," she says.

Although the U.S. Bureau of Labor Statistics doesn't offer employment projections for personal shoppers, they do predict that jobs for retail salespersons (a starting point for many would-be personal shoppers) will increase 10 to 20 percent between 2002 and 2012.

As a personal shopper for a retailer, your clients are the store's customers. You will establish relationships with them and keep track of their important dates (birthdays, anniversaries, etc.).

Whenever they need something, you will shop within your own store to find the perfect item – such as a gift, a business outfit, or an accessory for their home – then coordinate everything involved in the purchase, including any alterations, gift wrapping, and delivery.

Unlike a straight sales position, you are not expected to staff cash registers and make yourself available on the floor to serve customers. You are expected to communicate with customers and to make every effort to set up appointments convenient for them.

5

Working for a retailer is such a fabulous job that some personal shoppers stay in the position for many years. An example is Betty Halbreich, who was Bergdorf Goodman's personal shopper for over 20 years, helping celebrities, executives, and other clients find the perfect outfits.

1.1.3 Benefits of a Career in Personal Shopping

There are many reasons why personal shopping is an excellent career choice. The benefits of a personal shopping career include:

No Formal Education Is Necessary

While many personal shoppers have related training or education, generally no degree is required to become a personal shopper. No special education, experience, or connections are needed to get started and succeed. (In this guide we will show you how to get experience, and explain how to make connections.)

Low Cost to Get Started

Unlike other occupations that can cost thousands of dollars to enter, you can become a personal shopper no matter what your current financial situation. You can even start your own personal shopping business at home with few or no upfront expenses. If you have access to transportation, a computer, and a phone – you have all you need to get started.

Booming Industry

Retail is a multi-billion dollar a year industry and opportunities for personal shoppers are increasing every year. According to the National Retail Federation, GAFS sales (general merchandise stores, apparel stores, furniture and home furnishings stores, electronics and appliances stores, and sporting goods, hobby, book and music stores) grew 6.7 percent in 2004, the highest retail sales growth since 1999. They predicted a continued growth rate of 3.5 percent for 2005.

In particular, the "luxury sector" is expected to thrive in the next few years, as high-income families are less affected by slow income growth and higher energy prices. In addition, the weaker dollar is increasing the demand for luxury purchases by tourists. All of these are potential target markets for the ambitious personal shopper.

High Income Potential

If you start your own personal shopping business you can earn up to $50 or more per hour, depending on your location and clientele. Some of the personal shoppers you'll read about in this guide earn $500 or more per day. If you are a personal shopper working for a large department store, your base pay may be supplemented or fully comprised of commission on sales. The more (and more expensive items) you sell, the more you make.

Opportunity to Build Good Relationships

Becoming a personal shopper gives you the opportunity to build good relationships with your clients and with your vendors. You'll get thank-you notes and calls (of course, you have to give those as well), and some of your relationships may turn into friendships.

Flexible Schedule

Personal shoppers work by appointment. Although they must be available when the busy people who use their services can fit them in (e.g. lunch times or either very early or very late in the day), they can often develop a schedule with a great deal of latitude.

A Typical Day For a Personal Shopper

A personal shopper's day might begin with an early meeting with department store buyers to find out what is coming in for the new season. Then the shopper would check phone messages and attend to anything that came up in those messages. She might:

- Have a coffee meeting with a client who is interested in having you help him purchase an engagement ring

- Confirm for a client that her new business suit's alterations have been done

- Call two or three clients to let them know their favorite cosmetic company is hosting a seminar at their boutique on Saturday morning they may want to attend

- Send a thank-you note to a client who has given her a referral that turned into more business

- Spend an hour in a shoe store looking over its new seasonal stock, and taking notes

- Work with an up-and-coming fashion designer to arrange an exclusive showing of the designer's new line (called a trunk show) for the shopper's client base

As you can see, personal shoppers have busy but varied days. Often the nature of their work depends on their own interests. Even within a retail employment setting, personal shoppers have a great deal of leeway to create their own job.

If a personal shopper has a particular interest in event planning, she can offer to get more involved with the marketing or publicity department in planning such things as fashion shows. If her interest is in fashion education, she may be able to convince her employer to help her set up a series of seminars at the local high school. Later in this guide you will find many ideas of exciting activities you can do as part of your career.

If you start your own personal shopper service, you will have even greater leeway to set your own hours and days of work. While you may decide to sometimes work evening or weekend hours to accommodate clients, you can take "time off" whenever you want.

Make a Difference in People's Lives

Few other jobs allow you to constantly create win-win-win situations. Your clients win, the organizations you shop with win, and you win. Winning is not, however, the only name of this game – joy might be a better term. As a personal shopper, you'll create joy for all the clients you serve.

Remember how it felt the last time a recipient of a gift from you got that look of total pleasure on their face? It was one of the most gratifying experiences on earth, for you and for them. As a personal shopper, you'll have the chance to recreate that experience over and over again all year long.

Interesting Job with Opportunities to Learn

One thing you won't be as a personal shopper is bored. You'll be constantly learning about trends and what's coming onto the market in the near future. You'll get to know all items carried by retailers in your area.

More than that, you'll get to know what accessories go with what outfits, or what add-on pieces of home décor go with which bedroom suite and so on. Even if you work for one particular store, you've also got to know what competing stores offer, and why your products and services are better for your clients.

Opportunity for Advancement

While personal shopping is itself a dream career, it can also be a stepping-stone to another fabulous job. Once you're a successful personal shopper, many avenues for branching out will present themselves. You are only limited by your own imagination and desire.

For example, if your specialty is purchasing home furnishings, you may find yourself interested in becoming certified as an interior decorator. A single corporate gift-buying job could lead to full-time work within that corporation. Many personal shoppers expand their businesses to include errand-running or image consulting services. It's even possible that you could get hired exclusively by a celebrity to make all his or her purchases, from outfits for public appearances, to pool equipment, to PDAs.

1.2 Inside This Guide

The *FabJob Guide to Become a Personal Shopper* is arranged to take you step-by-step through getting started and succeeding as a personal shopper. These steps, and the chapters they appear in, are as follows:

Chapter 2, Getting Ready, covers important preliminary steps to prepare you for becoming a personal shopper. Here you will discover the skills employers and clients are looking for, and the best ways to develop your skills and learn personal shopping.

Chapter 3 offers advice on How to Be a Personal Shopper. This chapter explains the steps involved in personal shopping and how to do them. It also explains how to find and choose vendors (companies that supply products and services).

Chapter 4 focuses on Getting Hired. If you want the security of a full-time job, this chapter will give you information to help you get that job. You will discover who hires personal shoppers, how to find job openings, how to prepare a resume, and how to do well in an interview.

When you're ready to Start Your Own Business, you will find some good advice in chapter 5. You will find practical information on setting up your office and getting ready to open for business, including setting your fees. In chapter 6, you will discover practical tips for Getting Clients.

The guide includes many insider tips generously shared by successful personal shoppers. You will also read about the experiences of a variety of personal shoppers, including the success story of a woman who has shopped for a princess, a personal shopping business that charges hundreds of dollars an hour, and a personal shopper who is paid $1,500 per day to take clients on shopping trips to Paris.

By applying the information in this guide you will be well on your way to your own fab job as a Personal Shopper!

2. Getting Ready

Before you begin applying for personal shopping jobs or start your own personal shopping business, it's a good idea to take some preliminary steps to prepare yourself for success.

This chapter begins with a quiz to help you begin thinking about your particular interests, skills, and knowledge related to personal shopping. That should give you a sense of areas you may wish to specialize in. You'll then discover how to develop specific skills and learn more about the profession. In the next chapter, you will get step-by-step instructions for actually doing each of the tasks involved in personal shopping.

2.1 Self-Analysis Quiz

While a great many of us love to shop, personal shopping as a career involves more than scheduling a pleasant morning with friends at the mall, followed by a leisurely lunch at a quaint restaurant. Your answers to the following questions will give you a better indication of areas you may want or need to develop in order to become a professional personal shopper:

Self-Analysis Quiz

	Yes	No
1. Do you love gift-giving?	❏	❏
2. Do you love dressing stylishly?	❏	❏
3. Do you often note whether others are dressed well?	❏	❏
4. Do you think of changes that could make them look even better?	❏	❏
5. Do you do that with people's homes?	❏	❏
6. Have your friends commented on your good taste?	❏	❏
7. Have your friends asked for your help with their wardrobe, decorating, gift-giving, or planning a special occasion for a loved one?	❏	❏
8. Do you pay attention to the little details that set one outfit apart from the run-of-the-mill, make one room into a showplace, or make a dinner into a feast?	❏	❏
9. Do you regularly read fashion magazines, home magazines, lifestyle magazines, or gift catalogs?	❏	❏
10. Do you watch television shows on fashion, antiques, decorating, or luxury lifestyles?	❏	❏
11. Do you ever watch a shopping channel?	❏	❏
12. Can you spot fashion trends?	❏	❏
13. Do you keep up on lifestyle changes, always knowing when there's a new popular gourmet food, or a new popular wine, or even a new popular restaurant?	❏	❏
14. Do you get enthusiastic when talking about these things with others?	❏	❏
15. Have you ever sold anything?	❏	❏

	Yes	No
16. If you have sales experience, did you enjoy it?	❑	❑
17. Do you enjoy meeting people?	❑	❑
18. Do you find it easy to get to know someone over the phone?	❑	❑
19. Do you enjoy helping others get what they want?	❑	❑
20. Can you get along with, and even enjoy, most people even if they are very different from you?	❑	❑
21. Can you accept the choices of others, even when those choices would never be yours?	❑	❑
22. Do you find it relatively easy to ask people for things?	❑	❑
23. When someone does you a favor, are you generous with your thanks?	❑	❑
24. Are you comfortable conforming to the expectations either of your employer or your clients?	❑	❑
25. Are you willing to schedule your time to meet the needs of others?	❑	❑
26. Do you like to multi-task? In other words, do you like a day filled with a variety of tasks, from the functional to the very creative?	❑	❑
27. Do you have a good memory for detail, or a good system for keeping track of things you want to recall?	❑	❑
28. Do you make "to do" lists?	❑	❑
29. Are you able to be spontaneous and take advantage of good opportunities, from great sales to the chance to meet interesting people on the spur of the moment?	❑	❑

If you're attracted to a career in personal shopping, you've probably answered yes to the majority of the above questions. Still, there may be some questions to which you answered no. As long as you have 75 percent or more positive answers (i.e. as long as you answered "yes" to at least 20 questions), you can become a very successful personal shopper by developing any skills you'll need, or by focusing on the areas that you have the greatest interest in.

2.2 Areas of Specialization

From answering the quiz on the previous pages, you may have noticed a particular area that you most enjoy learning or giving advice about. If you set up your own business, you could offer personal shopping services of all kinds, but specialize in a particular niche. You may also be able to find a full-time job in that niche. For example, toy retailer FAO Schwarz hires personal shoppers, and furniture retailers such as Ethan Allen hire "designers" whose job is very similar to that of a personal shopper.

You could choose to specialize in any area that interests you, and if there are enough people willing to hire you to buy those products or services for them you could create a successful business. On the next few pages you will read about specializations in personal shopping, so you can decide which one is right for you, then chapter 3 will give you instruction and tips on how to shop for each of these specialties.

Fashion

Personal shoppers who specialize in fashion are in high demand. As a fashion specialist, you will be expected to be familiar with the latest styles and trends. You must also know how to put together a complete outfit, including shoes and accessories. As mentioned in the previous chapter, personal shoppers in the area of fashion may also do image consulting, or advice on the client's overall look.

Food

While everyone needs to eat, not everyone has the time or ability to get to a grocery store. Your service could be as basic as shopping for weekly groceries, or you could locate hard-to-find specialty items in markets or online.

In some cases, personal shoppers offer a hybrid food service of personal shopper and personal chef – increasingly desired by busy families. You would shop for ingredients for six or seven days' worth of meals, prepare them, bring them to the client's home, and leave instructions for the prepared foods, and notes about what should be served with them.

Gifts

A few stores employ personal shoppers just for gifts. Tiffany & Co., the venerable New York City-based upscale jeweler, is one. Tiffany's offers tabletop selections, too, including fine china, crystal and silver. Their personal shoppers do a lot of gift advising for weddings and other "state" occasions. If you work for yourself, you can build a specialty in buying flowers, wine, or fine gourmet items.

Buying corporate gifts is another fabulous specialization for a personal shopping business. No matter what is happening in the economy, business owners and executives give gifts to show appreciation to their customers and suppliers. You may also be hired to find the perfect gifts to acknowledge employees.

How a Corporate Gift Buyer Created a Win-Win-Win

A Baltimore corporate gift shopper's business declined slightly after September 11, 2001, because people were sensitive about appearing too joyous in the aftermath of the terrorist attacks. So she put her talent and knowledge to use for everyone's good.

Some of her clients decided to send charitable donations in the name of their employees, clients and vendors. She explained to them how much more lasting their gesture would be if, instead of informing everyone with a memo, they did it on a lovely hand-painted card with non-sectarian wishes of goodwill.

Although her biggest sales time of the year diminished, it didn't disappear. And it turned out that her thoughtfulness about it was appreciated; her clients gave her a lot of business after the first of the year, at a time when it would ordinarily have been slower.

Home Furnishings

If you love making homes more beautiful, home furnishing and accessories is an excellent area to specialize in. If your work goes beyond simply shopping – if you actually go to clients' homes to assess the décor and suggest rearrangements and purchases that would improve the look – you can call yourself an interior decorator as well as a personal shopper. (Unlike becoming a certified interior designer which has strict requirements including two to five years of post-secondary education, you can be an interior decorator immediately.)

Electronics

With the overwhelming array of electronic products on the market, and the choice of buying by phone, online, or in person, there is an increasingly growing niche for an electronics specialist. People want advice purchasing these big-ticket items, but don't necessarily trust that the retail staff are educated enough to help them make the right decisions. If you are already a bit of a "techie," consider using your talents to shop for electronics for your clients. With the speed these products break down at, you'll be in business for a long time to come.

Other Specializations

Children's Goods

With so many dual-income families, those who love both shopping and kids products have figured out that this is an up-and-coming niche. If you have shopped for one or more kids of your own, you've probably already developed skills in selecting clothes, toys, and furnishings for young ones. Best of all, kids keep growing, so there's always more shopping to do.

Online Shopping

Like electronics, the Internet can be very overwhelming to the average person. Potential clients may be well-informed enough to know that they can make purchases online, but not web-savvy enough to find what they want and make the purchase. If you are an expert in online shopping, consider a shopping service for online products. Your client base would not be limited by your geographical area, only by your connection speed.

Personal Concierge or Assistant

Similar to personal shopping, this niche involves offering a wider range of services to your clients. If you are a personal concierge or personal assistant, you may take care of buying clothing, household goods, and gifts, but you will also do other services for clients, such as receiving deliveries, overseeing household repairs, arranging theater tickets, scheduling appointments, making dinner reservations, booking rental cars, and so on. Other terms for this type of service are "errand" or "personal assistant" services.

Seniors/Disabled

If you don't live in a thriving fashion center but still have an interest in personal shopping, consider a shopping service for seniors and people with disabilities. While you may not be able to charge as much for your services, these clients are often the most grateful for your help, and you will be truly helping people in need. Your services may include helping to read tags and labels, arranging transportation, and sometimes just chatting.

Tourists

If you live in an area frequented by tourists, why not offer a shopping service to them? The visitors could book a day of your services in advance, and you could lead them around to the best and/or often overlooked shopping places in town. If you can offer a local's perspective on touring the town for great deals, consider this specialization for your business.

Vacation Planning

This involves working with local travel agents, airlines and hotels. You need to know what various sorts of people might want in a vacation. They could book Disney World themselves, but if you can offer unique travel itineraries and put together all the bookings an individual or family would need, you've got it made in the shade. Related to planning vacations is planning unique "experiences." For example, you might plan a dream date for a couple's anniversary.

2.3 Important Skills

There are a variety of skills that can help you succeed as a personal shopper, no matter what your specialization. Even if you answered yes to each of the questions in the self-analysis quiz, it will not hurt to reinforce the skills you will need. Following are important skills used by personal shoppers. In section 2.4, you will find a variety of additional ways to learn these particular skills.

2.3.1 Customer Service and Sales

As a personal shopper, excellent customer service will be part of your job on a daily basis. You will need to determine your client's needs and ensure those needs are met. To be truly successful you will go the extra mile for your clients, keeping track of each client's important dates and calling to remind them of occasions they may want to purchase gifts for.

You will find many tips for developing customer service skills throughout this guide, particularly in chapter 3. You can also find many excellent resources on customer service online, including the articles at **www. CustomerServiceManager.com**.

While customer service skills are essential in this career, it is important to remember that your ultimate goal is to sell. You may have sold goods or services in the past, or you may be involved in selling now. However, personal shopping goes beyond what most people think of as sales. It is "relationship" selling, and it depends not only on the goods that are available, but on the way you treat clients, their perception of your interest in them, and your ability to hit the mark when presenting options to them.

Relationship selling, which used to be called consultative selling, demands that your sales skills add value to whatever the customer is buying. Part of the fun of using a personal shopper is that the shopper knows what sorts of things the customer likes and doesn't like, and pre-chooses only those things that will be appealing. It is often a foregone conclusion that the customer is going to buy. That being the case, your task is to give advice on the best of the possibilities.

In section 2.4 you will find ideas for learning sales skills used by personal shoppers. There are also many excellent resources (books, tapes, seminars) if you want to improve your relationship selling skills in general. A few websites with helpful tips on selling are **www.dexaquote.com/ topics/help.asp?topic80.txt** and **www.money.howstuffworks.com/ sales-technique2.htm**.

2.3.2 Purchasing and Product Knowledge

There are three main points to remember about being good at purchasing. Purchasing well is getting what you want, when you want it, at a price you want to pay. You can remember it this way: what, when, and how much.

Purchasing skills will be particularly useful if you go into business for yourself. But even if you are employed by someone else, you will need these skills. Integral to purchasing is knowing that you are getting the best buy for your money. "Best buy" means not only a good price, but also built-in value and suitability to the need the product or service is to fulfill.

Within each store, there are bound to be various price and quality levels for just about every product carried. When you select items for your customers, you need to know which items or services offer the quality/ price point that make it the best deal for the customer.

That means you will have to know those factors so well that you can weigh the customer's budget, expectations, use for the product or service and any other significant factors against what's available... and sometimes recommend a lower priced/lower quality item because it fits the bill. So, you'll have to know more about the products and services you deal with than your client. Indeed, this purchasing knowledge is a large part of the value of a personal shopper.

You can learn a great deal about purchasing from vendors if you take the time to cultivate good relationships with their representatives who serve you. They will often take the time to tell you things they don't tell their other clients, such as, "We did get a shipment of silk blouses in last week, but I don't think the seams are generous enough for your customers. Why don't I send you a sample of last year's blouses that we have left and see if one of those styles would work. They're better quality than this batch, and I can give you a discount because they need to be sold."

If you are self-employed, you will obviously need to know purchasing inside out. This begins, naturally, with educating yourself completely about the products on the market in each area you deal with. In addition, being able to tell your customers about the origin of the products and services you recommend is a selling point for your expertise.

For example, if you are dealing with clothing, you will need to know whether items were manufactured in the U.S., Canada, Europe, or a third world country. Because some of your customers will be sensitive to employment practices in third world nations, you won't want to present items that they may later find were produced in unacceptable conditions. If the item was mass-produced, it could also lack quality.

You will learn more about purchasing later in this guide, particularly section 3.2 (*Working with Vendors*). There are also many resources that have information on purchasing, plus fashion resources to help you develop your sense of style, in the Resources section of this guide.

2.3.3 Organizational Skills

If you have superb organizational skills, you've got a leg up. To be a personal shopper, you need to be able to organize everything, so even exceptional organizers might need to add some tricks to the magic they do. Here's a list of what you'll need to organize your time for:

- Meetings and consultations

- Studying trends in your industry's products or services

- Checking out stores and manufacturers that make things your clients might use

- Shopping

- Packaging and/or arranging delivery

- Paperwork

- Follow-up

- Promotional duties, networking, etc.

- Special events

- The unexpected

Some people like a physical daytimer; others like to make a schedule on their computer and download it to a Palm Pilot. Whatever way you choose to do it, be sure to set up a reminder system a day or two ahead of important events or tasks. You might also consider color-coding blocks of time that will work every week for various tasks.

For example, if you know that Tuesdays between 10:00 a.m. and 1:00 p.m. is the best time to meet with your store's buyers to see what will be coming in, block it in throughout your calendar and change it only in emergency situations. If you block in ahead of time all the "must do" activities each week or month, you will not be tempted to accommodate customers in ways that cause you either stress or a loss of valuable information. You will have automatically limited the number of hours you will work.

Granted, in the beginning of a job or a business, you probably will put in some extra hours to learn and to develop your clientele. But those extra hours should be productive ones, not ones caused by putting too many entries into your calendar to handle and still get the essential tasks done. It will work best if you consider some of your time – whatever you determine to be essential – to be "sacred," and able to be changed only for a real emergency.

2.3.4 Negotiation

If you're employed, your negotiating skills will likely be used primarily in-house, to make sure the buyers are aware of the items you need so they can purchase accordingly. However, you will probably also need to negotiate with clients from time to time.

If you're running your own business, you will negotiate prices with vendors of items you want to purchase for your clients. You may also negotiate a variety of other matters, such as advertising rates for your business, office equipment and supplies you purchase, wages for people you hire, or the rate charged by the credit card company you use to buy items for your clients.

One of the classic rules in negotiating is that you must be willing to walk away from the deal if it doesn't suit you. You can probably do that if you are running your own business, however, you may not have that option if you are employed.

You may be able to use shipping as a way to hone your negotiating skills and gain savings as well. When you buy items at retail prices, you might be able to negotiate to lower your costs and impress your clients with your "connections" and some small savings for them. Most of the room for negotiation is found in shipping costs. When you have made a good number of purchases from a single vendor, even if you are still buying at retail, speak with them about absorbing or at least sharing shipping fees. After all, you are bound to be one of their best regular customers, not only bringing them sales but expanding their brand recognition and goodwill as well.

If you want more information about how to improve your negotiating skills, an excellent resource is the book *Getting to Yes: Negotiating Agreement Without Giving In,* by Roger Fisher, William Ury, and Bruce Patton.

2.3.5 Ability to Spot Trends

As a personal shopper, clients will turn to you not only for your advice on which products provide the best value, many will also want to know what is "hot". For example, an aunt may want to know which toys her nieces and nephews would love for Christmas, while a client who works in a creative field such as advertising may want to ensure the clothes they wear to work make them look like they are on "the leading edge."

To spot trends, you've got to know about any breaking news that could have an effect on what your clients will desire. Did today's hot rock star just determine that spandex capris were "in"? They won't work for your larger clients, but you'll have to know how to get "the look" for them in styles that are flattering... and sometimes, you'll have to sell them on more appropriate items and you'll have to do it so that they're thrilled when you've finished.

As a professional personal shopper, you will naturally want to read industry publications so you can be among the first to know about upcoming styles and trends. Industry associations often conduct research to identify consumer preferences. For example, the International Council of Shopping Centers, the trade association of the shopping center industry, has an annual list of "hot gifts" in toys, clothing, food, books, electronics, jewelry, home furnishings, and other gift items.

Sometime before the holiday season starts to approach, check out the Holiday Watch website by the International Council of Shopping Centers at **http://holiday.icsc.org**.

You will find other resources that can help you spot trends in the Resources section of this guide. These resources include websites, associations, and publications that give insider advice about industries such as giftware and apparel.

2.4 Ways to Learn Personal Shopping

The great thing about this career is that you can decide yourself how you want to go about learning the skills. If you are in a position to go to school, you can take fashion merchandising courses, but you can also learn without taking any formal courses. You might take a workshop or two, read books and websites, or if you have some free time, try to work within the retail scene to make contacts and learn the products.

In the next chapter of this guide, you will get step-by-step instructions on How to Be a Personal Shopper. In the meantime, here are some other ways to learn the business.

2.4.1 Observe Other Personal Shoppers

Observation is often the best teacher. Choose a department store you like to shop in and make an appointment with the store's personal shopper for your next purchase — for instance, a business suit, shoes and accessories to go job-hunting in for a position as a personal shopper. You'll find out several things, including:

- How long it takes to get an appointment with the store's personal shopper. (Even before that, you'll find out how long it takes them to call you back.)

- Whether there is an additional charge for the service.

- How long it takes them to pull together items for you to see

- What sort of information the personal shopper gathered about you, and how he or she asked for it

- The way you were treated by the personal shopper

- The surroundings: an office, a comfortable lounge, and so on

You might do the same thing at two or three stores and compare all those factors. By doing that, you'll know what you could improve on if you were hired in a similar position, or if you decide to begin an independent business of your own.

2.4.2 Window-Shop

Here's where the fun begins: you get to actually go to stores! A lot. Take notes about unusual items you see and ask sales associates for more information.

Jot down the manufacturer information about lines of merchandise that you like. If you are going to be an independent personal shopper, it is sometimes possible to buy directly, passing on the savings to your customers (which will help create even greater demand!), or at least to find out quickly and easily later on where to get what you think your clients will want.

When you go "research shopping," prepare a notebook ahead of time. Consider getting a 5x7 wirebound notebook with section dividers, or use the Vendor Information Form provided on the CD-ROM that comes with this book. You'll want information such as the following to go on each page:

- The date

- The store

- The department

- The purpose of visit

- Items of interest (a two or three word description)

- Where it was made

- Anything else the sales associate can tell you

Then create a separate page for each item you want to recall and give a full description of it, including size, colors, care instructions for clothing, the weight if it needs to be shipped... in short, anything you or your client would need to know when considering this item.

TIP: This is something you will do to increase your general market knowledge. When you look for specific items to fulfill specific needs of your customers, you will create similar notes. Those notes will include only the items you have pre-selected to present for your client's choice. And they may be much more detailed than your background notes.

2.4.3 Information Interviews

An information interview is a meeting with someone to learn about their job. To arrange an information interview, contact personal shoppers through referrals, online, or even the Yellow Pages. Explain that you are studying personal shopping as a career and ask if you can arrange to meet with them for 20 minutes to ask a few questions. People are much more likely to agree to a meeting if they know it won't take too much time.

Unless you have a personal referral, personal shoppers who work for department stores and other large retailers may redirect any requests for information to their publicity, corporate communications or public relations departments. But there are exceptions, and you won't know until you ask.

Even though they are busy people, some hiring managers will give you some of their time. Susan Olden of Saks Fifth Avenue says she loves talking to young people and sharing advice: "I've talked to a lot of young people and I'm more than happy to do it."

Olden also says that the more informed a candidate is about the nuts and bolts of the business, the better they'll interview, the better experience they'll acquire and the better employee they'll eventually become — it's a win-win for everyone.

Owners of personal shopping businesses may also be willing to speak with you, but be aware that they may not be eager to help if your plans are for a similar service in the same locality. Or they may decide they could use some help and try to hire you!

If you are going into a niche they do not serve, they might be more willing to tell you how they built their business. But don't expect hard numbers about how much they earn; if they are not a publicly traded corporation required by government regulation to report their financial information, they have no need to tell anyone except the tax collector. Still, you will get a sense of their earnings by their surroundings, their vehicles, their business equipment, how often the phone rings as you talk and so on.

In addition to any other areas you want to learn more about, here are some things you could ask them:

- What hours they work and how flexible those hours are

- How much of their time is spent shopping or surveying stores or departments within their stores, how much is devoted to research and keeping up with the latest trends, and how much is devoted to other tasks

- The non-financial rewards of doing what they do

- What they like most, and what they like least, about their career choice

- Any challenges they experience and their tips for dealing with them

- What advice they wish someone had given them before they started

After the meeting, make sure you send a thank-you note and, if someone referred you, thank that person as well.

2.4.4 Donate Your Services

Acting as a personal shopper for friends and family is a great way to develop your skills. You may not be able to charge much – if anything – for your time and expertise. But you can sharpen your eye, improve your skills, and collect letters of appreciation to get you started.

Volunteering is another good way to learn your business and help others with the business of life. One great place to donate your time and skills in return for the joy of helping and the opportunity to learn is to a Dress For Success program near you.

Dress For Success is an organization that helps unemployed women get back into the workforce by providing resume and interview help and, most importantly, a free or extremely low-cost starter business ward-robe. Because the apparel is donated, you'll have an excellent opportunity to use your creativity to make outfits that work for clients who need your help more than any of your private clients ever will... and who will probably appreciate it more, as well.

You might also have the chance to hone other skills such as negotiation in asking stores for donations. Check out their website at **www.dress forsuccess.org**.

2.4.5 Work Experience

If you have more time than money, another good way to get related experience is by taking a part-time job for a company involved in a related industry. Even if the job doesn't focus on shopping, it can give you an opportunity to learn valuable skills that could help with your job hunt.

One of the easiest ways to get this kind of experience is by applying for a part-time retail sales job. Many retailers have high rates of staff turn-over, so they are always hiring. While the starting pay won't be high, you can get the kind of experience that employers and clients look for.

While any type of retail experience can be valuable, the types of retailers that can best prepare you for a personal shopping career are those that sell the products your clients are most likely to hire you to shop for, such as clothing, gifts, home furnishings, etc. If you have the opportunity, look for a position where you will have an opportunity to learn about the products you sell.

For example, some retailers offer training programs to help their employees develop their sales skills and learn more about the merchandise they carry. Even better, if you hope to move into a full-time personal shopping position, is to get an entry level sales position with a retailer you would love to work for as a personal shopper.

Another way to get experience is by working in a call center, or customer contact center. These positions involve working on the phone or by email to assist customers with their purchases. (Avoid call centers that deal only with customer complaints.)

For example, makeup company Sephora has "beauty advisers" who will help customers select beauty products by phone or computer. As mentioned earlier, some companies actually use the title "personal shopper" for these positions. Even if the job isn't true personal shopping, having this title on a resume can certainly help you stand out. Like retail, customer service positions typically have high turnover, so you will probably find many positions advertised in your local newspaper and online.

Yet another option is to consider working in any capacity for a manufacturer of the types of products you would be buying for future clients. This may give you an opportunity to learn inside information about how the products are manufactured.

2.4.6 Resources for Self-Study

The next step in educating yourself is reading books and periodicals in the field. Publications for consumers can give you some good ideas, but they generally will not contain cutting-edge information. You can get an excellent grasp of current trends in your field by reading periodicals for the retail and gift industries. This knowledge can not only be helpful while you're working as a personal shopper – it can help give you an advantage over other applicants.

The Resources chapter of this guide has information and links to an excellent selection of periodicals, books, industry associations, and web sites.

2.5 Education

As mentioned in the introduction, no formal education is required to become a personal shopper.

However, having some educational credentials can make a good impression on both employers and clients. Susan Olden, who hires personal shoppers for Saks Fifth Avenue, says education is not a requirement for personal shoppers at Saks but does say relevant education will certainly raise her eyebrows.

2.5.1 Degree Programs

According to Dr. Sharon Pate, coordinator for apparel merchandise and design at Illinois State University, if you majored in Fashion Merchandising, Sales, Marketing or Business Management in college, milk it for everything it's worth.

Higher-level positions (for example, if you want to move into management) typically require university degrees and if you have one going into the position, that gives you a leg up over the competition. Some of the larger retailers offer tuition reimbursement to its employees, so if you lack a degree once you get hired, it's still possible to get one after.

If you are interested in getting a degree, it can be helpful in a number of ways. Consider the following:

- What you learned in school, a non-college-educated employee will have to be taught. Pate says that at ISU, students take classes ranging from cultural diversity in fashion to marketing, merchandising and problem solving. The less time an employer has to spend training an employee in these areas, the better.

- Most college students will get internships. This is the best way to get practical experience you can use to demonstrate to a prospective employer that you can do the job. Some internships pay, and some don't. But if you do an internship well, the worst thing that can happen is you can get a good letter of recommendation.

- It will serve you well if you decide to start your own personal shopping business. Being self-employed is a one-person show. It means you will take care of all aspects of your business, accounting, billing and so on. You can learn all about that in college.

A recent search at Petersons.com found 53 universities and colleges in the United States offering programs in Marketing Operations (a category that includes Fashion Merchandising, General Retailing, and General Sales Skills and Operations). To search for colleges, visit **www. petersons.com** and look under the major "Marketing Operations."

2.5.2 Continuing Education

If you decide you'd like to take some formal coursework, courses in the following areas may be particularly useful:

- Fashion

- Merchandising

- Purchasing

- Retailing

While many colleges offer degrees or diplomas in these areas, you might consider simply taking one or more evening courses. (Virtually every college and university has a department offering continuing education programs.) If you would like to earn a diploma through home study, one program that includes a personal shopping component is Professional Career Development Institute's fashion merchandising program. Tuition is $589 (a payment plan is available) and you can complete the 17 lessons at your own pace. Visit their website at **www.pcdi-homestudy.com/ courses/fm**.

In addition to courses on the topics listed above, it can be helpful to take any adult education course that improves basic skills related to personal shopping. Following are examples of the types of subjects that may impress an employer or help you in your career:

- Business

- Communications

- Customer Service

- Computer Skills

- Home Decorating

- Image Consulting

- Negotiation

- Time Management

- Sales

Different programs will have different titles for their particular courses, but after reading this chapter you should have a good idea of the types of classes that will be most useful to you. You may find classes on color, style, wardrobe – even gift giving (most likely to be offered before the holiday season) or shopping.

For example, the Boston Center for Adult Education offers a class on creating a stylish wardrobe on a budget. And once you feel confident in your knowledge of personal shopping, you might even consider teaching a continuing education class! (If you're interested in teaching people how to shop, see section 6.3.2.)

3. How to Be a Personal Shopper

3.1 Personal Shopping Services

Whether in a retail setting or working on their own, a full-service personal shopper will likely perform at least these basic types of activities:

- Help clients define their needs or wants

- Help clients determine budgets for their purchases

- Recommend specific purchases of goods or services

- Shop for or order goods or services

- Provide reminder services for seasonal or gift purchases

- Keep track of client preferences, sizes, etc.

- Handle delivery of items

The sections that follow explain how to do each of these things. Many of the examples involve working with clients in your own personal shopping business. However, much of this information will also be helpful if you are employed as a personal shopper.

3.1.1   Help Clients Define Their Needs

Before you can shop for someone, you have to know what it is they want. Sometimes they may not even know exactly what it is they want until you help them figure it out.

Since you're going to be a personal shopper, you already know you can talk with people easily and get to know them. But now you've got to be more specific. How do you begin? You haven't got two years to develop a relationship and find out your client is a birdwatcher and likes to send expensive chocolates to her daughter in college.

Instead, develop a checklist. On the pages that follow you will find lists of questions you can ask individuals and corporate clients. The CD-ROM that comes with this book has blank checklists you can print and use with your clients.

For Gifts

- What is the occasion?

- Who are the gifts for (e.g. family, friends, employees)?

- How many gifts will be needed in total?

- What date are the gifts needed for?

- Do you have any gifts in mind?

- What is your total budget?

- What is your budget per gift?

- Do you want the items to be gift-wrapped?

- Do you want a message included on a card with the gifts?

- Where do you want the gifts delivered?

- Should everyone get the same gift or will different gifts be needed for different categories of people (e.g. major clients, new clients, other clients)?

- What types of gifts have you given in the past?

- Did you receive any feedback about those gifts?

- Would you like your logo or company slogan to be included on the gift?

- What do you hope to achieve with these gifts (e.g. thank you, remember an occasion)?

- Is there anything that should not be purchased for any reason?

- After I bring you some gift recommendations, how long will the decision-making process take?

- What are the gift recipient's leisure activities, clothing preferences, favorite color to wear, size, etc.?

General Wardrobe

To assist you in choosing fabrics, ask the client questions such as: "In general, do you like natural fibers better than synthetics? If so, is there ever a time you would consider synthetics?" (The answer may be that the client would consider them for travel, as they are not as prone to wrinkle; in fact, you might even suggest that.) You may also discover that your client is allergic to particular fabrics.

Find out your client's favorite color to wear in each area of life. This is not just her favorite color. For example, a woman's favorite color may be yellow, but she may prefer wearing black business clothes, blue leisure-wear, and red formal wear.

For each of the above categories ask if the client has any preferences of brands, designers, or retailers. You should also ask whether the client has any particular dislikes.

If clients want you to purchase complete outfits, you'll also need to find out their preferences in accessories (belts, shoes, neckties or scarves, jewelry, etc.). If you will be shopping without the client, you will also need to know clothing sizes.

It may seem indelicate, but undergarments are another type of purchase you may be asked to make for your clients. This will more often be directly by women for themselves, but men may also ask you to buy lingerie for the woman in their lives.

Ask your client if this will be the case. If so, then collect size information and some information about preferred manufacturers or stores. For example, many women like Victoria's Secret, but would rather have less romantic items in their closet, especially for business and sports.

When you are filling in the blanks in your questionnaire and developing a complete profile of each client's preferences in things for themselves and for gifts, remember to take note of anything unusual about their preferences.

And don't be afraid to ask for specifics; in fact, ask for all the specifics you can get. Your client might not tell you that when she does wear skirts, she refuses to wear heels. This information is important, so when you hear that she prefers pants, ask if she ever wears skirts, when, and what length. In this case, she might say, "I only wear skirts when I can wear sandals. Or sometimes, I'll wear a mid-calf velvet skirt with a silk blouse to an important event, one that sort of indicates no pants."

From this, you might determine that she does not like pantyhose, and avoids wearing them. You would also discover that she doesn't like high heels (remember the rule: the longer the skirt, the lower the heel). You would make notes to remind yourself of this in the appropriate place on her Client Information Card (for ongoing clients).

Business Wear

Here are some questions you could ask to determine what the client wants in terms of business attire:

- What is your profession?

- What dress is expected? (Business? Business casual? Casual? Other?)

- Do you work in this climate always, or travel? (For example, if you live in Florida and the client travels for business in Thunder Bay, Ontario, you're going to have to consider winter clothing for her at some point.)

- In business attire, do you go for a classic look (suits and significant jewelry), trendy (whatever's in the fashion mags now as "new" acceptable business attire), or natural (minimal jewelry, neutral colors, natural fabrics)?

- What are your favorite fabrics to wear to work? (If your client is not familiar with fabrics, ask if she prefers soft fabrics, sturdy ones, smooth or rough ones.)

Leisurewear

Once you have a list of their preferences for business attire, make a similar list for their leisurewear. People's hobbies and lifestyles both have an effect on the sorts of clothing they will need while they are not at work.

You will want to ask questions such as:

- Do you have children? How many? What ages? (If the client has young children, activewear in very washable fabrics is likely to be important to her. If her children are older, she may need clothing to join them in some of their activities, such as tennis, going to the theater…or just about anything.)

- What sports do you play, or help your children with? What sports do you attend? For example, if the client attends mainly amateur or pro football games, a wardrobe of jeans, attractive tops and jackets will be essential. If you don't know what is the expected spectator attire for a particular sport, ask. Then do research on your own to come up with interesting versions of the expected attire.

- What are your other leisure activities? (This could run the gamut from reading books – where no particular attire is required – to going on safari, in which case you will be getting familiar with outdoor outfitters in a big way.)

Formal Wear

You should also ask about your client's preferences for formal wear. Find out whether they attend formal dinners or other events that require formal wear, and how many such events are attended each year. As with business wear, ask if the client has preferences for particular fabrics.

With formal attire, people tend to spend a lot of money and yet only wear the outfit or the dinner jacket occasionally. In the case of a gown, usually a woman doesn't want to wear it to more than one function in a year. You can be valuable to your clients by showing them how to get a high-fashion look for these items without paying a high-fashion price. The bulk of their clothing dollars are better spent on the items they use again and again, such as good business suits and shoes.

How can you find the high-fashion/low-price combination? Two ways. Keep tabs on the stock at your local department stores, and know when they have sales on designer clothing. And build relationships with designer knock-off retailers and wholesalers who can give you the look without the price tag. You will get advice on how to find some of these retailers later in this guide.

Home Products

- How many people live in the home?

- Do you have children? What ages?

- Do you entertain frequently?

- What are you looking to purchase?

- Why are you purchasing this item?

- What is your budget for this purchase?

- Do you prefer beauty, function, or a mix of both?

- How much use will this purchase get, on a scale of 1 to 5?

- What colors do you decorate in where this item will be placed?

- What decorating themes do you prefer for the area?

- Do you have a specific manufacturer in mind?

- Do you have a specific retailer in mind?

- What are the features you prefer this purchase to have?

- What are the features you prefer it not to have?

- Have you purchased this item in the past? Were you satisfied with it? How could it have been improved?

- Are there any size restrictions for this purchase?

- Any other details to assist in selection?

Food

In addition to the questions below, you can have your clients fill out a full shopping list. A checklist will save your clients time writing things out, and many grocery stores offer aisle-by-aisle checklists for you to use that will save you time too.

- How many people live in the home?

- Do you have children? What ages?

- Do you entertain frequently?

- What is your budget for this purchase?

- How long should this food last?

- Are there any dietary restrictions I should be aware of?

- Are there any food allergies in the household?

- Do you have a preferred vendor?

- List types of fruit you like to eat. What is your favorite fruit?

- List types of vegetables you like to eat. What is your favorite vegetable?

- List types of meat you like to eat. What is your favorite meat?

- List types of dairy products you like to eat. What is your favorite dairy product?

- List types of grains you like to eat. What is your favorite grain?

- Is there anything you are craving lately?

- What foods should I never purchase for you?

Client Information Card

When you have a client who will use your services on an ongoing basis, you can then put together a profile about your client. Here's a sample Client Information Card for a client named Mrs. Really Busy. (If you work as a personal shopper for a retailer they will have their own form.)

Sample Client Information Card

Contact Information

Name:	Mrs. Really Busy (prefers to be called Bizzy)
Address:	13 Fast Lane, Austin, TX
Phone:	(555) 888-1234
E-mail:	MrsRB@email.net *(home)*
	MrktngGenius@biznet.com *(work)*
Profession:	International marketing consultant, self-employed

Business Attire

Work attire:	Suits, preferably pants for lots of flying.
Climate:	Usually temperate in U.S. and Europe; sometimes tropical or subtropical.
Fabrics:	Prefers natural fabrics such as silk, wool and cotton. Slightly allergic to wool – can only wear if lined or mixed with other fiber. *Does not like synthetics.*
Favorite color to wear:	Black, sometimes chocolate brown, and some beige in summer.
Style:	Classic, although will also wear trendy things on occasion. Likes natural fabrics. Prefers pants to skirts, even in tropics, for business clothing.

Leisurewear

Children:	None
Participant sports:	Tennis, riding horses
Spectator sports:	Tennis, football
Other activities:	Attending theatrical productions and symphony; attending fund-raisers, usually black-tie affairs.

Other Apparel

Travel:	Frequent, business. But often weekends at the business destination. Sometimes must attend black-tie affairs on trips.

Lingerie:	Prefers to buy own, except for bathrobes. Only likes terrycloth robes for winter; short cotton men's kimonos for summer.

Gifts

Personal:	Has one elderly aunt; a male companion who lives in another city; her horse trainer; several female friends; her brother and sister-in-law and their child, a little girl.
Business:	Several vice presidents of companies selling products internationally. Must be gender-neutral. Must not be anything like a "logo item" or "advertising specialty" and must not be something they can see at Tiffany's and check the price. But must be Tiffany-quality.
Personal Gifts:	Birthdays, anniversaries, other special occasions client will tell me on a case-by-case basis.

Schedule For Gift-Giving

Person	Date	Notes
Aunt	December 1	Eyesight not good
Male companion	May 15	Has *everything*
Brother	October 2	Likes to golf
Sister-in-law	June 30	Likes to cook
Niece	December 15	Child, will be 10 this year; ballet dancer, artistic
Friend Judy	April 1	Writer with 3 young children; too busy!
Friend Bertha	July 24	Loves to travel and read
Friend Don	September 3	NASCAR enthusiast; also red wine connoisseur

Business Gifts:	Likes the same winter-holiday gifts sent to all on or about December 7. **NB:** Don't call them Christmas gifts; she does international business, and there are varied religions her clients practice. Gifts should not look like "Christmas.")

3.1.2 Help Clients With Their Budgeting

Budgeting for a Single Purchase

If you are working with a client on a specific purchase, they will usually have a spending limit in mind. You can then check with vendors (see section 3.2) to determine what your client can get for that amount.

> **TIP:** Remember that your fee will have to be included in the total cost. Information about fees can be found in section 5.4.4.

However, there may be times when a client does not know what is a reasonable amount to spend on a purchase, and asks for your advice. If they have a general idea of the type of gift they want to give, you will be able to give them an indication of cost after checking with a few vendors. After you've been a personal shopper for a while you may be able to give your clients estimated costs without checking with vendors first.

You may need to give advice even if your client does have a specific figure in mind. For example, if your client's daughter is getting married, she may think she needs to spend $1,000 for a mother-of-the-bride dress. Maybe she does. By sitting down with her and determining whether the dress will be useful for other occasions and events, you may decide together whether $1,000 is fine or whether you can help her save money on that purchase (remember the designer knock-offs!). Then you can use the extra money to improve other parts of her wardrobe, or to use for gift purchases.

Your task is partly to help your client take the "bad" emotion out of buying ("I should overspend on an outfit for my ONLY daughter's wedding!) and put the "good" emotion into it ("This less expensive dress looks great, and if I never wear it again, so what? Now I can afford those designer winter boots I've been wanting. I can wear them when I fly out to Denver to see my daughter and her husband in their new house.")

To best advise your clients on their budget, you'll need to keep in mind their overall plans for the year. Sometimes, helping clients determine a budget for a single purchase is reminding them that if they spend too much on one item, they will not have enough left in their budget to complete the wardrobe they need for next season, or the accessories for their new Great Room, or whatever is in their on-going purchase plans.

If you are employed by a company, you will likely be provided with various forms and tables that you will need to complete for each customer and sale. And the company's accounting staff will be available if you get hung up on any part of it. But if you are in business for yourself, you may have to sharpen your budgeting skills.

Fortunately, many good accounting packages are available for home computers, and they virtually all come with tutorials. You can find more information about keeping track of finances in chapter 5.

Annual Budgets

Many clients seeking your help (though not all of them) probably earn a substantial income. They may also be seeking your help after realizing some of the clothing or gift purchase dollars they spent in the past have been wasted — or at least that they haven't provided maximum value.

The first thing you need to do to help your client budget is determine whether they prefer to make small but frequent purchases, infrequent major ones, or something in between. It is unlikely that a client will reveal to you everything about their income and budget overall. But you can ask them: What is your clothing budget this year? If they don't know, ask how much they spent last year and ask if they are planning the same or more.

You can also take this opportunity to remind them that even though they may pay something for your services and expertise, the added value of the items and their appropriateness for the purpose they are meant for, plus the time savings, will give your client more value than they purchased with the same dollars last year.

When you have that figure, you can ask how they like to spend it: in monthly, quarterly, semi-yearly or yearly increments. Most likely, they will want to spend some of their clothing dollars before the beginning of each new season.

But ask them if they are interested in buying extra things, beyond their budget, when after-season sales begin. Some clients will not be interested at all, especially if they are trendy types. But classic and natural dressers, for example, may find it wise to reserve some of their clothing dollars for that purpose.

All this could be noted on the Client Information Card you create, which could also contain billing and payment information. (You can find more information about arranging for payment in section 5.4.5.)

3.1.3 Recommend Specific Purchases

Purchases Suggested by the Client

Sometimes clients will have a specific item in mind that they would like to purchase. Unless they are set on the item, you may want to give them some alternate suggestions if you do not feel the product is a good one. Here is an example of what you could say:

> "Mrs. Weiner, you mentioned that it's important to your mother to provide good care for the two birds she has adopted from the humane society. Although she wants to have a birdcage in her aviary so the birds have a secure place to rest at night, I don't believe your mother will be satisfied with the quality of the birdcage you are mentioning, even though she did find the ad for it.
>
> What about spending a little more to buy a birdcage that almost cleans itself? We could shift a few things around, or even take advantage of pre-season sales for the children's school clothes. A better birdcage would be so helpful to your mother now when she's watching the children for you after school. And a few years from now, it might become difficult for her to remove the tray from the cage unless it's really light and easy, like it is on the Bird Heaven model."

The example above is one in which the personal shopper might suggest not only a specific purchase, but also a particular brand. Each time you work on a project for a client, such as "Winter Wardrobe for Self, Daughter, 2005," you will recommend specifics as part of the project.

Recommending New Purchases

When might you recommend purchasing an item or a service when the client has not suggested any purchase? Let's go back to that Client Information Card and add one more bit of information:

Wants to be notified of sales of items usually purchased.

Of course if you are employed as a personal shopper with a retailer, you will contact your clients whenever you have a sale or new items in stock that may interest them. If you have your own business, you will be keeping tabs on the sorts of things your clientele usually purchase. If you are smart, you will develop relationships with sales associates at the stores where you often purchase.

To do that, when you first shop for a particular item ask for the sales associate who is most knowledgeable about that item. Give him or her your card, and explain that you are a personal shopper and would be very happy to have help, as they know the store's merchandise better than you do. These days, most sales associates have cards because the stores know shoppers may build a relationship with them and become more loyal customers of the store.

Because you are a professional shopper, they will be even more interested in having you as a frequent visitor/buyer. Have each sales associate from whom you receive a card write on it his or her usual days and hours of work so you can plan your trips. When you return, try to work with the same associate again.

Ask the sales associates you usually work with to call you if something they think would suit your clients comes in, or if a sale is coming up. As long as you place your purchases with them, most will be more than happy to let you know.

In these cases, however, you would recommend a specific purchase only after reviewing your Client Information Cards and the questionnaires your client has filled out. You can also transfer some of the details you get back in the client questionnaires to a Client Project Card, which would be a page or so of notes on a specific purchase.

TIP: Make duplicates of each Project Card. File one with the Client Information Card, and the other in your weekly to-do files. When you check your projects each morning, you'll know what items you still have to find to recommend, but you will also have that information available when you review Client Information Cards before talking to a client.

Stand up, Give a cheer
Maddie's big day is here!
Friday, November 18th
4pm -7pm
111 Ninth Street
Regrets only
201-933-5611

OK. Let's go back to the Client Information Card again. It's gift time! And you have the firm impression that no ordinary objects will do for Mrs. Busy's dear friends and family. (Actually, you asked how important it was to her that gifts be unusual, and she said, "VERY. EXTREMELY.") You got the point and wrote that on her card. So now you've got to fulfill her dreams. You get to spend lots of time learning all sorts of product lines from all sorts of vendors of gift items and items that make good gifts.

3.1.4 Putting the "Shop" in Personal Shopper

Sometimes shopping will be as easy as picking up the phone or going online and ordering the item that you know is perfect for your client. Other times, you will need to shop around to find the best vendor.

Before you shop, you should educate yourself about products that are currently available. While you can refer to resources such as those listed in the final chapter of this guide, you can get a tremendous amount of information "in the field". Spend a couple of hours each day in stores looking at merchandise or talking with sales associates and, when you can, the store's merchandise buyer. To speak with the buyers, you'll have to make an appointment, and you may have to be persistent. They are busy.

Buyers can give you valuable advice on upcoming products. For example, the big couture shows in Paris happen in the beginning of October. Right after that, buyers will be looking at what the designers have shown, and where they can get copies or lower-priced similar outfits, or the designer off-the-rack line for their stores.

You might drop them a note before they leave (if they go) in late September, wishing them a good trip and telling them you'll be thrilled to hear what they have to say about the spring season when they've gotten back and caught up a bit.

In addition to shopping at retailers, you may be able to get discounts on merchandise by buying it from a wholesaler, or directly from the manufacturer. Section 3.2 gives detailed information about your different options for buying products and services.

3.1.5 Provide Reminder Services For Purchases

Providing a reminder service for seasonal and gift purchases is important both for your clients, and for you. It is one of your best marketing tools. It is a way to increase and plan your own income streams, but it is a bona fide, needed and appreciated service for your clients.

If you are employed as a personal shopper with a retailer, they will have a reminder system already set up. However, if you have your own personal shopping business, you will have to create your own system.

Some appropriate seasonal reminder times (times your clients are more likely to shop) may include the following, as well as the occasional events listed at the end:

- Valentines' Day

- Winter Vacation/Getaway

- Spring Break

- Easter

- Spring/Summer Wardrobe

- Mothers' Day

- Fathers' Day

- Summer Vacation

- Fall/Winter Wardrobe

- Back to School

- Thanksgiving

- Halloween

- Hannukah

- Christmas

- New Year's Eve

- Birthdays

- Anniversaries

- New Baby

- Housewarmings

- Weddings

- Religious Ceremonies

For reminder notices, create a Monthly Reminder File. Into each month's folder, you will place reminders to yourself to remind your clients of something. For example, you know that three or four of your clients are refurbishing a house. You have bought a few accessories for them, and you know a few more who have expressed an interest in upgrading their linens "sometime." So put in a note to yourself to do two things in December:

- Call the local housewares/bedding/department stores you work with and check the online outlets about upcoming January white sales

- Drop a card to each client who would benefit, asking them to call you about getting "white sale" items

In July, you would remind yourself to check up on a few things, like upcoming school fashions, fall women's fashions, off-peak travel bargains (and travel fashion bargains!), and fall gourmet food items for gifts.

Then, of course, you would drop a postcard or e-mail to the appropriate clients. If you send a postcard, follow up by phone to be sure the client got it. Open a discussion about the upcoming season, event or client needs, as appropriate. If you e-mail, you can send them a "return receipt," just like postal letters. Usually, those elicit responses. But if you get no more than the automated response back from one or more, pick up the phone and call them.

Do this for each month, with the appropriate merchandise and service categories for the following month. This will allow you time to do your research and set appointments with your clients to discuss their needs and begin projects.

3.1.6 Handle Delivery

Chances are that some of the items you buy will need to be delivered. For example, if you purchase something that is custom made, it may take several weeks or more to have the item shipped to you.

The shipping fees may be included in your purchase price, but ask the salesperson if you are unsure, and get an estimate of the charges if they are paid upon delivery.

Large items you may order for a client – an inflatable raft for an outdoorsman or a sofa for a client's new Florida room – will best be delivered to the client. You may need to arrange to be at the client's premises to accept delivery, and unfortunately, you will probably only get a "window of time" (e.g. "sometime between noon and 4:00 p.m."), not an exact delivery time. You will need help to unload large items, as well, as this is not the job of the truck driver — they're paid to drive the truck. You may also have to arrange for assembly of some items.

Be sure to note any obvious damage to the shipping box or item on the delivery form when you sign, and inspect the item carefully. Items are sometimes damaged in delivery. If you have not purchased shipping insurance, the delivery company will only pay you a portion of the item's value, based on its weight.

Purchasing insurance will cover the true value of the item if it is damaged in shipping, but not if the manufacturer packaged it improperly. In that case, you want to deal with the manufacturer directly.

With smaller items, consider having them shipped to you instead of the client. While you may be tempted to ship the items directly to your client (called "drop shipping") for convenience, if there is a mix-up or damage, your client will not be happy to deal with it — that's why they hired you. Better to play it safe and have the items shipped to you to be signed for and inspected prior to delivery to the client, so you can deal with any surprises.

Since you will likely be spending a lot of time away from your office, it may not always be convenient to wait for deliveries. If you live in an apartment complex with a manager on site and run your business from there, it is often possible to arrange for the manager to accept deliveries.

If you rent office space, you can usually get these services from the front desk if it is a big building, or you may be able to make arrangements with an adjacent office that is staffed continuously. In fact, the possibility for getting deliveries when you are not in should be a consideration before you sign a lease on office space.

If you live in a single-family home and operate your business from there, you can arrange a drop so that you don't have to wait for deliveries or risk their disappearing while you're out shopping for someone else. One possible arrangement is a pre-fab storage shed in a carport or around back. Install a lock, but also create a chute big enough for packages to slip through and a revolving bin for large parcels. Or, in some cases, you can arrange for the delivery service you use most (probably UPS and FedEx, as those are the ones your vendor is likely to use) to have a key or the combination. There may be some items that are too big to leave this way, but most will work fine.

If you do arrange a drop, either like this one or with a residential manager, you'll have to provide documentation for the delivery service before they will drop parcels without a signature. You might also want to arrange some extra insurance for your premises to cover anything that might go missing this way.

Delivery of Clothing

If you are shopping for your client at local clothing stores, it is likely that you will pick up and deliver the items so your client can try them on for approval. If alterations will be needed, it may be preferable for your client to visit the store. And if the store doesn't do alterations, you might have to arrange those, as well. If you can snag a tailor willing to come to your client's home or business to do the fittings, so much the better.

After all, the reason your client contracts for your services is for convenience and time savings, as well as your style-price-quality-planning expertise. (Whew! Did you know you were all that?)

TIP: If your clients are buying expensive clothing meant to last for more than a season, it will be worth it to them to have them properly fitted. As you plan your business, make sure you know a reputable professional tailor to do any alterations. Because tailors are often overbooked, take the time to find one who will be willing to perform work for you as soon as it is needed; you can assure the tailor that he or she will have continuing work from you, and the opportunity to work with some excellent garments. You can also ask the tailor to teach you about garment construction.

3.2 Working With Vendors

As a personal shopper you will likely buy a wide variety of products and/ or services for your clients. The companies you will buy from are known as vendors. If you are employed by a retailer, you will primarily be working with a single vendor (your employer). However, educating yourself about the industry may help you stand out when you are searching for employment, and will very likely be handy to know when you are on the job.

In this section you will learn about different types of vendors, where to find vendors, and how to work with them to get the best deal for you and your client. This section concludes with a "case study" showing how you might track down a particular product.

3.2.1 Types of Vendors

Retailers

Retailers are companies that sell direct to the public. These vendors include department stores, shoe stores, home products stores, gift shops, florists — just about any sort of store you can find in the mall, even supermarkets and specialty shops. These days, retailers also include businesses that operate online.

A list with links to hundreds of major retailers in the United States and Canada is available at **www.ecr.ryerson.ca/retdev_04.html**. They are broken down by category, such as clothing, food, gifts, housewares, jewelry, toys, etc.

Shop Top Ten (**www.shoptopten.com**) also has links to retailers in a variety of categories. Clicking on each category will take you to a page full of links to companies in that categoy. If you don't mind looking at flashing ads, you can find discount coupons so you can offer your clients not only expertise, but sometimes a better price. For instance, clicking on the Clothing link turned up special deals at Coldwater Creek, Eddie Bauer, PacSun and more.

Wholesalers

A wholesaler buys products from the manufacturer, usually in large quantities, and resells them in smaller lots to retailers. As a result, the wholesaler is sometimes referred to as the "middleman" between retailers and manufacturers.

If you will usually be buying items one piece at a time, you probably won't use wholesalers much, unless they also sell retail. You are more likely to work with wholesalers if you buy large quantities, such as dozens or hundreds of a unique gift item for a corporate client.

If you are buying large quantities, you will get the best deal if you can buy directly from the manufacturer. However, some may not be willing to sell to you because of their arrangements with their current wholesalers. In those cases, you will need to go to the wholesaler.

You can find wholesalers in the Yellow Pages under whichever category you are looking for (e.g. Giftware). Another option is to check directories at your local public or university library. For example, while you could buy the American Wholesalers and Distributors Directory for $250 from the publisher (Gale), chances are you can find this or other directories at the library. Of course many wholesalers can also be found online.

Here are some links to lists of wholesalers.

- *Yahoo Directory of Wholesalers*
  Links to scores of wholesalers.
  http://dir.yahoo.com/Business_and_Economy/
  Business_to_Business/Wholesalers/

- *FarCountries.com*
  Offers giftware, home décor, and more from 30 countries, and it is "to the trade" only. So you need a resale certificate (see section 3.2.3) in order to access it.
  www.farcountries.com

- *BasketBizHelp.com*
  A collection of over 700 vendors that specifically cater to the Gift Basket industry. $18.95 for a resource guide and wholesale directory, or $9.95 for the wholesale directory alone.
  www.basketbizhelp.com/1resources/whsledir.shtml

Manufacturers

Manufacturers are companies that make products, usually in large quantities. Most manufacturers sell to wholesalers, and will not sell directly to individuals.

Thomas Register is the most comprehensive online resource for finding manufacturers in the United States. At their website (**www.thomas register.com**), you can do a search by company, brand, or product (e.g. "clothing," "gift" or "jewelry"). Each manufacturer's information includes the head office address, phone number, fax number and product descriptions.

The *American Manufacturers Directory* includes detailed information on over 600,000 U.S. manufacturers. While you could purchase it your-self for $795, you will probably be able to find it at a local university or public library. Many libraries carry directories for specific industries as well.

If you specialize in a particular area, you may eventually want to purchase that industry's directory of manufacturers. However, directories typically cost several hundred dollars, so you may want to view them at the library first, if possible.

For example, the *Canadian Apparel Directory*, published by the Canadian Apparel Federation, is available on CD-ROM for $350. It includes listings of menswear, womenswear and childrenswear manufacturers and designer-manufacturers. Listings include telephone, fax, address, brands, and complete product information. In addition, contact names, numbers and e-mail addresses are listed for the President and sales contact for each firm. If you would like to know more about this directory, visit **http://bookstore.apparel.ca**.

In the U.S., apparel manufacturers can be found through the *Directory of Brand Name Apparel Manufacturers*, which is available for $115 at **www.fashiondex.com/mfg**. You can also see a free online list of links to apparel manufacturers through the American Apparel and Footware Association Membership Directory at **www.americanapparel.org/ 4col.cfm?pageID=103**.

Check the Resources chapter of this guide for more professional associations and industry publications.

Contractors

Contractors are businesses or self-employed individuals who do work such as renovations, house cleaning, etc. If you provide concierge services, you will likely have a core of contractors (they may also be called subcontractors) you can call when a client needs something done.

Even if you don't offer concierge services, you may sometimes need to find people to provide particular services. For example, you might need to hire an artist to paint a portrait of a client's husband as an anniversary gift. You can find information about working with contractors in section 5.3.2.

3.2.2 Choosing Vendors

You probably already know the reliability of local department stores you might use, and some specialty shops as well. And with well-known vendors like Bloomingdale's or L.L. Bean, you can usually be assured of service and quality so you can pass those things on to your clients. But what about smaller retailers or wholesalers that don't have a national reputation to uphold? Or those who supply you with specialty items? The fact that you are dealing with a large, national company doesn't mean things can't go wrong.

Buyers sometimes have to deal with manufacturers' "over-runs" or "under-runs," changes in style, changes in price, delivery problems and other unnamed glitches. A good purchasing agent can overcome those to a great degree. And, if you want to properly serve your clients, that's exactly what you'll do.

In order to minimize any problems, you'll have to qualify vendors before you deal with them. If they don't measure up after you've gone through the questions in this section, you may still need to use them if they are alone in their field and you need them for a particular client's buys – but at least you can deal with it if you know what to expect.

When you are considering buying from a new retailer, spend some time speaking with the owner or manager. With wholesalers, speak with the sales manager. With manufacturers you will likely speak with a sales representative.

You will first need to ensure that a particular vendor can actually supply what you need. For example, if you are buying an item for one of your individual clients, find out if the wholesaler or manufacturer can handle single or small orders.

If a company says they can provide what you need, here are the types of questions you'll need to answer in order to "certify" a vendor for your purchases.

> **TIP:** Get answers to these questions for at least two vendors of every single type of item you expect to purchase, and do it as soon as you can. You won't have information about every vendor when you set up shop, but if you specialize in women's fashion, for example, you should at least know the major business attire, leisurewear, outerwear, accessory, leather goods and underwear retailers and manufacturers you will use. If you are planning on room makeovers, know the policies of the major local shops you will purchase from, as well as the national chains like Pier One and Internet/mail order retailers like Domestications.

Quality

Can this vendor provide the quality of products I need? As well as asking for product specifications and instructions, ask to see samples to determine quality. While pictures of products can be helpful, they have often been photographed in a studio. In "real life" they may not look nearly as good.

You also may not have the opportunity to take photographs yourself. For example, furniture manufacturers will not allow photos to be taken at their showrooms. If you need to let a client see an item before you buy it, find out if you can try out an item "on memo" (on loan) for a few days. (If not, you can often get swatches or samples.)

If you are dealing with a retailer, will you be able to arrange holds for your clients so they can run in and try things on or look at them at their convenience? Will the retailer also let you take items "on approval" for your clients to look at?

Getting Items "On Approval"

If you shop regularly at some stores, and these stores realize that you are in business to stay and that you contribute income directly to their bottom line, they may allow you to take items "on approval" for your customers. You may have to leave a small deposit or possibly your credit card information with them, in case you fail to return the items at the agreed-upon time or your client decides to keep them.

This sort of arrangement can work very well for you, because, for one thing, it saves your cash flow. For another, it lets your client know how well-thought-of you are by those retailers.

And also, they know they would probably not have the opportunity to try out merchandise without paying for it in full, necessitating a full refund and all that entails if it was not perfect for them. So cultivating these relationships is a win-win situation for you and both your client and your vendor.

Prices and Terms

Are the prices and terms the company is offering acceptable? Ask the vendor to tell you all the charges that will be involved with a purchase. In addition to the price of the product, there may be taxes, delivery charges, duties for items coming from another country, rush charges, etc. If you are dealing with a wholesaler, you should ask about "upcharges" (a fee on top of the manufacturer's price).

What discount will you receive off the retail price? Typical discounts when buying wholesale (i.e. from the manufacturer) are 20-50%. Section 3.2.3 explains how to qualify to buy wholesale. You may even be able to negotiate a discount of 10% or so with some retailers by explaining that you are a personal shopper and can bring them additional business.

Will the company accept returns, preferably without a restocking fee? Ideally, you want to be able to take things on approval and return them if they didn't suit your client. If not, however, ask about negotiating return fees and shipping charges. You can charge your clients shipping for things they buy, but they are unlikely to be pleased about paying for shipping on things they don't buy. So you'll have to absorb any of those costs unless you work out a deal in advance with each vendor.

If an item is special ordered (for example, if you have selected the upholstery for a sofa), chances are you will not be able to return the product once it is delivered to your client's home. However, some stores will allow returns if you pay a restocking fee.

A restocking fee is normally a percentage of the original purchase price that is paid to the store to take back the item for a refund. An average restocking fee is 10-15% (however they can even range from as little as 5% up to 25%).

When is payment required? If you do not have a business history, most vendors will want to be paid for items before they ship them. Sometimes, though, they will ship items to a major client of yours without payment in advance if that client has a good credit history.

For instance, if you were to recommend buying 50,000 yo-yos for a Fortune 500 company open house giveaway, it is likely the manufacturer would ship them to the Fortune 500 company, and bill them for the yo-yos. You would have to then bill the Fortune 500 company separately for your fees, but it would save you from finding financing for 50,000 yo-yos.

While you can use a credit card for retail purchases, many times you will not be able to purchase wholesale using your credit card, so you will need to have funds readily available to cover your purchases with a check.

What about over-runs or under-runs? While manufacturers normally do their best to ensure they deliver exactly what you have ordered, many include in their contract that they can ship 10-15% over or under the amount ordered. Personal shopper Ilene Mackler describes how she handled an under-run:

"I did a job for a company in Florida. The company ordered pewter beer steins and needed 165 for a convention they were having. I got a letter from the manufacturer saying they had only been able to ship 151, as the others didn't meet their quality assurance standards. You have to know this: when you order from vendors, they usually retain the right to ship 15 percent under or over because of mistakes. But that didn't help me or my client.

So I called the company and asked how bad those other mugs were. I begged them to find fourteen more that were acceptable. They called back and said they had found fifteen that they were willing to ship, but because they didn't stand behind the quality of those, they couldn't in all conscience charge full price, so those would be forty percent off.

So I called my client, told him what happened and said he could have the other few mugs at 40 percent off. I assured him, from what the manufacturer had told me, that it was unlikely anyone would see anything wrong with the naked eye. He was happy. Now, I could have just charged him the full rate for those 15 mugs. But that wouldn't have been fair. And my integrity is important to me."

Ethical Issues

Clients are increasingly concerned with ethical issues involved in the production of goods. Some questions you can ask to determine if a vendor is socially responsible include the following.

- Does the company know where imported goods come from?

- Are they manufactured according to human rights standards?

- Can the manufacturer certify that their products have not been tested on animals?

- Is the manufacturing process environmentally friendly?

If a sales representative claims not to be able to find the answers to these questions, you should assume that the company does not meet the ethical standards your clients will expect.

Ethics also extends to the company's business practices with clients. For example, will they fulfill your orders in a timely fashion and not let them be delayed if larger orders come in?

Your Representative

Will I be served by one representative? Or, if I buy over the telephone, can I request one representative and build a relationship with him or her? (Except for very small purchases, like accessories that cost less than $50, it is probably wiser to order by phone than over the Internet. That way you can ask any questions you might have, and you can find out if there is a large stock of a particular item that you think might appeal to more of your clients.)

If you are not hitting it off with a rep, will the company assign a different one? (In an ideal world, you could get along with everyone. But it's not an ideal world, and getting the service you need so you can serve your clients is an essential part of purchasing.)

Warranties

What warranties are provided? Warranties, when provided, are normally a form of insurance that your client will get some or all of their money back if there are any defects with the item. Make sure that both you and your client are fully aware of what is being warranted and how long the warranty is good for (one year is the norm for any defects, except "as is" items normally not covered under warranty).

Additionally, the warranty might state that the consumer is responsible for paying the cost of shipping the product back to the manufacturer to fix any defects.

References

Has the company provided names of satisfied customers I can contact to check out what I've been told? In addition to checking references, you should do your own research, both online and with the Better Business

Bureau, to discover whether there are any potential problems with the vendor.

Developing Relationships

Once a vendor has answered these questions to your satisfaction, you can add them to your list of preferred vendors. But beyond simply keeping this information on file, develop relationships with vendors you expect to be working with in the future.

If you have clients with special needs or unusual sizes, try to arrange for buyers at retail stores to inform you first when those items arrive. Why would they be willing to do that? Because it almost certainly means a better chance of selling those things than if they didn't tell you and left it to chance that you would find them, or some other person who needed them would find them.

Popular toys are sometimes impossible to get... unless you have developed a good relationship with the vendor. Bear that in mind. Because, although the major children's gift holidays come but once a year, they can be crucial to your clients, and therefore crucial to you.

After you have done business with a retailer or wholesaler for a while, you can apply for a line of credit. If the rest of your credit picture is good, both personally and professionally, you may be granted a small line of credit, subject to increase if all goes well.

3.2.3 How to Buy Wholesale

As a personal shopper, you may be able to get substantial discounts by buying wholesale. By buying wholesale you will typically pay 20-50% below the regular retail price. You can either pass these savings on to your clients, or mark the price up. (See the section on fees for more information about your options.)

Purchasing wholesale lets you see the latest products before they are available to retail consumers. However, rarely can you bring your purchases home the same day. If your client needs something right away, you may have to settle for retail that time around, or investigate the possibility of purchasing "floor models" or items on display.

What You Must Have in Order to Buy Wholesale

To be able to purchase items at wholesale prices, you will need to show evidence that you are an industry professional. For example, if you want to purchase furnishings, you will need to show that you are a professional interior decorator.

TIP: Personal shoppers who specialize in shopping for products for the home can call themselves *interior decorators*, if they wish. No special education or certification is required for this designation – unlike the designation *interior designer* which does have strict requirements in many areas.

In the U.S. you will typically require three things to be admitted to industry events and purchase wholesale: a business license, business cards, and a resale number. These items are all covered in chapter 5 (*Starting Your Own Business*). The resale number is also known as a tax number, a resale permit, or a sales tax permit. You are required to show this number on a certificate (use a photocopy) when you want to shop wholesale.

Where to Buy

Trade Shows

A trade show is held in a convention center or exhibition hall, featuring booths that people can visit to learn about different products and services. While some shows are open to the public, the ones you should attend if you want to buy products at wholesale prices are trade shows for specific industries, such as apparel, gifts, home furnishings, etc.

Trade shows are held in various locations throughout the year. One of the best ways to find out about upcoming trade shows is through the industry publications and organizations in the Resources section of this guide. Many trade shows are also listed at websites such as **www. tsnn.com** and **http://tswstg.cahners1.com/index_tsea.asp** which let you search for events by industry and location.

Admission is sometimes charged to get into these shows, and a few have prior purchasing requirements, but most should be free and accessible when you show your credentials (see below). Guests are sometimes welcome as well, although they will not be authorized to buy. The common discount at these shows is 50% off retail, although wholesale will usually be the marked price.

You may find trade shows to be the perfect opportunity to network within your industry, as they often have social events in conjunction with the day-to-day buying and selling. Some will also offer seminars on business topics that may be of interest to you.

Factory Showrooms/Outlets

These are not retailers you see at malls that call themselves "factory outlets" (but actually offer little or no discount), but are true outlets or showrooms located by the manufacturer's factory that feature their products exclusively. For example, there are factory outlets for hundreds of furniture brands, including Drexel Heritage, La-Z-Boy, Thomasville, and many others.

With smaller factories you may find that no outlet or showroom exists, but you can arrange a meeting with a salesperson to look at samples, place orders, or purchase the older sample items. In this setting, it is very important that you respect the supplier's time and environment, since you are not their major source of income. When you are ready to buy, let a salesperson know, and they will place the order and arrange for shipment.

If they require you to be a "stocking dealer," this means they require a considerable minimum purchase. If you are still set on one of their items, ask them to refer you to one of their wholesalers (where you will likely have to pay a mark-up fee).

If you are nowhere near the factory you want to purchase direct from, but know the item you want, they sometimes will allow you to place an order by phone. You will pay in advance and supply your credentials, and the product will be shipped to you.

Wholesale Design Centers

If you purchase home furnishings, you can find wholesale design centers in many large cities in the U.S. such as Boston, Dallas, Houston, New York, and San Francisco.

Calculating Your Discount

Although the cryptic numbers on sales tags are a mystery to most, there are really only three basic types of codes that are used in wholesale showrooms. You may question why these codes exist in the first place, but they allow you to shop with a client without having the client see your mark-up.

The 5/10 Code

When samples have tags that look like fractions, such as 50/35 or 60/55, this is known as the 5/10 code. To determine the wholesale cost, you subtract $5.00 from the first number in the fraction, and ten cents from the second number. So for example, an item that was tagged 80/60 would cost you $75.50. When dealing with furniture, the price is per unit; with fabric, it will be per yard.

Straight Discounts

If you do see actual prices rather than codes, and you are in an environment that allows decorators to bring clients with them, those prices are retail. Discreetly ask a salesperson what the decorator discount is (usually quoted in percents) then calculate the price based on that. If you are told the discount is "keystone," this is industry lingo for a 50% discount.

Compound Discounts

This type of discount is most often found when dealing with hard window treatment showrooms, and carries with it a deeper discount. The items will be tagged retail, and you will be told that your discount is a fraction, for example 50/20, or 50/50. To calculate what you will pay, you deduct each percentage in order from the amount. For example, to figure out a 50/20 compound discount on an item tagged $200, deduct 50% from 200 (200-100=100) and 20% from the remaining 100 (100-20=80). Thus, a 50/20 compound discount price on a $200 retail item would be $80.

Reprinted from the *FabJob Guide to Become an Interior Decorator*

There is usually no admission charge at a design center. Once you register at the front desk, you are free to explore within the center, which is a grouping of showrooms. If you plan to bring your client with you, they should register as such. Prices should be marked on items in wholesale codes that only you (and not your client) will be able to decipher.

Although most showrooms within the center will allow you to browse, some will require you to be accompanied by a salesperson. Design centers are becoming more public-friendly, and may have days you can enter without your credentials. Be aware, though, that the deep discounts rarely apply on these occasions.

As you start networking with other professionals in your industry, you will hear about a variety of suppliers in your community. In the meantime, you can check out **www.dezignare.com/designcenter.html** and **www. i-d-d.com/interior_design_centers.htm**.

3.2.4 Case Study – Find the Shoes

YOUR ASSIGNMENT: You need to find a pair of size 7 Stuart Weitzman pumps in red alligator for a client. How would you go about it? On the next few pages you will read what we came up with. However, you may want to try the assignment yourself first, so you can compare your own results with those of our researcher.

First, you should know what your local upscale retailers carry. It is likely you'll find Stuart Weitzman shoes at Nordstrom's. Call there first. Suppose the shoe department says they had some but are sold out in the size you need for your client. Ask them to call other Nordstrom's stores for you.

Still no luck. Size 7 is very common and shoes sell out fast, despite heavy ordering in that size. Now what?

Go to the Internet. Type "Stuart Weitzman" into a search engine. You'll get the company's website, and more. Save the "more" for later, in case you need it. Then go to Stuart Weitzman's website, located at **www. stuartweitzman.com**.

Use the site's search engines. Oops. No choices for red alligator given. Your client might have in mind a style from some years ago. But you've asked her what she really wants, and it's not so much the alligator as the color red, and she wants a dress pump.

Now go back onto Stuart Weitzman's site and search for red dress pumps. Still nothing. Go back and search by "use" – casual, sport, dress, etc. – and look at what Stuart Weitzman's current collection offers. Observing those shoes tells you that black and taupe are the main colors in the collection this season. Now what?

Go to the next site you found in your search: **www.shoes.com**. This is a big, discount search engine. But after searching by style, color, size and price range (all of them!), nothing turned up. Now what?

Lots of websites offer Stuart Weitzman shoes. So, choose one. (For this experiment, we went to Amazon.com, which most people think of for books and maybe CDs, but not shoes.) Amazon didn't have any Weitzmans in red. But broadening the search turned up this:

Hush Puppies® 'Angel' Pump
Nordstrom: $39.95
Usually ships within 1 to 2 business days

This is a mid-height plain business pump. But the client is looking for something dressier than that. OK. Search shoe accessories for something with a bow or other shoe decoration. Like this:

Vaneli 'Rhea' Pump
Nordstrom: $76.95
Usually ships within 1 to 2 business days

This is a business sling-back, with excellent detailing on the toe and straps. You could possibly present this to the client. And then there's:

Nickels 'Quirk' Pump
Nordstrom: $79.95
Usually ships within 1 to 2 business days

AHA! It isn't alligator, but it has excellent detailing on the toe, a two-inch heel and the pointed-toe look your client prefers. The price is excellent, and checking the availability chart on the Amazon/Nordstrom site reveals they can be shipped today in the proper size.

But what about the alligator aspect of the order? Keep looking, but be prepared to sell your client on the substitute, knowing it was really detail, color and pump style she was looking for.

Stuart Weitzman did make a red alligator pump back in the late 1980s. You could try to find a pair on a vintage clothing web site, such as those listed here:

- *Hemlock Vintage Clothing*
  www.hemlockvintage.com

- *Rusty Zipper*
  www.rustyzipper.com

- *Unique Vintage*
  www.unique-vintage.com

- *It's In The Past*
  www.itsinthepast.com

- *Just Say When*
  www.justsaywhen.com

TIP: The Internet has been a boon to vintage clothing retailers. When you are buying gifts or putting together unique wardrobes, it is handy to have your finger in this pie, too. Survey the sites, and e-mail the ones most appealing to you to inquire as to whether they would work with you on approval.

Most vintage sites, understandably, have an "all sales are final" policy. But if you're going to be a good customer for them, and introduce them to your market, they may be willing to make special arrangements with you. If they do, be sure to comply with their requests; they may ask for rapid decisions and quick return, or overnight shipping, etc.

Be sure you make these things known to your clients when you choose vintage items for them. Include in your contract that the client will pay for any additional freight or stocking charges incurred if they do not decide to return the item in the time allowed.

Or, instead of searching at vintage clothing retailers, you could just type "red alligator women's shoes" in a search engine. One of the results that might come up is **http://dmoz.org/Shopping/Clothing/Footwear/High_Heels**.

Wow! A directory of almost 50 stores that sell high-heel shoes! Look over the description for each store, and visit the stores that sound like they can help you the most. Say you end up clicking on a store called "Classic Pumps," which is located at **www.classicpumps.com** and is described as offering "genuine leather high heels in sizes 3.5 to 12."

You would find this:

Nany, by Pepe Jimenez/Amour
Description: Want to look your best and maximize comfort while you walk? Choose our Nany style, featuring our exclusive low-cut vamp, a 2.5" spike heel, leather sock lining, and long-wearing genuine leather "flex soles" that prevent slipping when you walk.

Yup, they come in red.

All shoes sold by Classic Pumps offer some "toe cleavage," which, according to money guru Suze Orman, is the only cleavage that should be shown around the office. (These are things you've got to know if you're going to advise businesswomen on their wardrobes, so read up!)

It only took a few minutes to find all that. But what about Stuart Weitzman alligator shoes from the 1980s? Well, while searching, say you run across a site called Nicole's Revival at **www.nicoles revival.com/acc.htm**.

Nicole's Revival has the very shoe, although in a different color and a half-size bigger:

Manufacturer: Stuart Weitzman
Description: Brown faux lizard heels
Size: 7.5
Price: $20

Would this pair work? For the price, you'd be foolish not to order them (after checking out the boutique's return policy) because if they fit at all, they could probably be dyed.

Few of your shopping assignments will take this much searching, but just imagine how great it will feel to find an item your client couldn't find on their own.

3.3 How to Shop For...

Maybe you are a shopping lover, but have not had the experience of purchasing the notably wide range of items that a personal shopper can be expected to produce (with speed and savings). Here are some general purchasing tips to guide you through each of the typical categories, along with resources to learn more.

Also, websites like the ones below allow you to compare online prices at a glance.

- *Epinions.com*
  www.epinions.com

- *NexTag*
  www.nextag.com

- *Shopping.com*
  www.shopping.com

- *Yahoo Shopping*
  http://shopping.yahoo.com

3.3.1 Gifts

You are going to be asked to find "unique gifts for people who have everything." Your client may have an item or theme in mind, based on what they know of the recipient. Clients will rely on your ability to discover unique, new, or hard-to-find items that will impress the person who receives it.

Likely Purchases

Collectibles, unique items, perfume, wine, jewelry, "themed" items.

General Tips

- Ask the cashier for a gift receipt for clothing, which allows the recipient to exchange sizes without seeing what was paid.

- Ask the store to gift wrap the item… many will do this if asked but won't offer. Don't forget the card!

- Find out in advance if your client is opposed to gift certificates.

- Match gifts with known interests of the recipient (sports, ballet, roosters, etc.)

- Buy generic but tasteful gifts for your client to keep on hand in case they are surprised with a "gift-giving" situation and need to respond quickly.

- If you are buying gifts for kids, ensure that the gift is age-and-development appropriate.

Quick Links: Buying Gifts

- *So You Wanna Buy Gifts People Actually Want?*
  www.soyouwanna.com/site/syws/gifts/gifts.html

- *How to Find Unusual Gifts*
  www.ehow.com/how_1705_find-unusual-gifts.html

3.3.2 Clothing

You may shop with or without your client along, and might shop for their wardrobe, their kids' wardrobe, or gifts for family and friends. Clients who shop with you will expect you to be more knowledgeable than them about fashion, and will look for your advice and ideas. Clients who let you shop for them may not be looking for the latest trends, but will expect you to be intuitive about their tastes and preferences.

Likely Purchases

Seasonal wardrobes, business wear, casual wear, eveningwear or formalwear, shoes, lingerie, accessories, clothes for young children.

Quick Links: Buying Clothing

- *How to Shop for Clothes*
  **http://fashion.about.com/cs/tipsadvice/
  ht/shopclothes.htm**

- *"Before You Buy" Index*
  http://fashion.about.com/cs/bb.htm

General Tips

- If you are wardrobe shopping, make an appointment to visit the client in advance so you can take some notes on his or her existing wardrobe.

- If shopping without your client, ask the retailer about bringing items to him or her on approval, with a credit card number as deposit.

- Get a list of preferred vendors from your client, in case the first choice is not available.

- Ask client to wear appropriate undergarments for the type of clothing he or she will be shopping for.

- If you haven't seen your client in a while, confirm sizes are the same.

- Check garments for loose buttons or poor sewing quality, especially with discount items.

- Plan to take breaks if shopping with a client for food and drink.

3.3.3 Electronics

Your clients will send you to purchase electronics because you are up-to-date on the latest advancements in technology. These are big-ticket items, so you will need to be savvy to succeed.

Likely Purchases

TVs, receiver/speakers, computers, cell phones, DVD players, PDAs, iPods, video game systems.

General Tips

- Ask not only what the product can do, but what it can't do. Your client may be thrilled with the portability of their new laptop, but not so enthused to find out that it has a two-hour battery life.

- Check out the website **www.epinions.com**, where consumers post reviews of all sorts of products including electronics. When the same complaint comes up again and again, it's a great way to spot a lemon.

- Find out warranty details before you buy. If the electronic device will be used for your clients' work, they may want to ensure they can get a loaner while theirs is being repaired. Ask the repair counter clerks what brands they see most often, and stay away from those.

- There is always room for negotiating price when it comes to electronics. Make sure they know you are a personal shopper and can bring them plenty of business, if they can get you a deal on price.

- If you can't get a better price, see if you can get some value added, in the form of accessories, high-quality speaker wire, software packages, etc.

Quick Links: Buying Electronics

- *Technofile's Gadgetry Guide*
  www.technofile.com/guides/buygd1.html

- *Ecoustics.com*
  www.ecoustics.com

3.3.4 Furniture

Furniture selections are normally made based on style and how a piece looks (whether or not it is aesthetically pleasing); however, comfort, durability and function are other important factors to take into consideration. Find out from your client what they value the most in their furniture purchase, and select accordingly.

Likely Purchases

Sofas, chairs, desks, coffee tables, ottomans, beds, tables, antiques.

General Tips

- Measure the space for the furniture in advance, so you aren't wondering how long of a sofa to buy, etc. In quaint, small spaces, you may want to measure the door as well, to make sure you can get the furniture in.

- Get details about the furniture before you buy, such as what kind of wood the piece is made of, what kind of finish it has, and how it was constructed, so you can inform your client.

- Inquire in advance if your client will want upholstered furniture treated to resist stains. While this may seem like a given, some clients could be chemical-sensitive and not want the treatment.

- Find out your clients' available hours for delivery in advance.

Quick Links: Buying Furniture

- *Furniture Buying for the Confused*
  www.furnitureadvice.com

- *Buying Furniture*
  www.buyingfurniture.com

3.3.5 Food

Busy people, seniors and the physically disabled are the clients most likely to ask you to shop for food for them. Busy people will probably just give you a list of preferences and send you off, while seniors and disabled people may shop with you, wanting your assistance reading labels and reaching items, and unpacking them at home.

Likely Purchases

Weekly groceries, specialty items, party fare.

Quick Links: Buying Food

- *NetGrocer.com*
  www.netgrocer.com

- *Lifetips Grocery Tips*
  http://grocery.lifetips.com

General Tips

- If possible, survey the client's existing supply of food to coordinate purchases with possible meals, or provide your client with a checklist a day in advance so they can just check off what they want.

- Make a note of any food allergies your client and his or her family have (e.g. fish, nuts, milk, or eggs) or dietary restrictions before you purchase, as well as preferences for organic, kosher, no GMOs, etc.

- If you are shopping for party fare, get the recipes in advance and make your list based on them.

- Part of the service you offer should be creativity: visit specialty stores, bakeries, delis, and ethnic food shops to keep your purchases interesting.

- As with your own shopping, check expiration dates before you purchase. You can make a list for your client of which items expire first, or advise them to arrange the fridge like a grocery shelf: with freshest in the back.

- It's a good idea to verify items purchased with your receipt before you leave them with the client, to resolve any discrepancies.

- If there is a local grocery delivery service, simplify your task and order online or by phone.

3.3.6 Housewares

If you are working with a client who is moving into a new home or re-decorating, you may be asked to purchase appliances and housewares. Elderly clients may also be overwhelmed with the selection of products, and need some guidance as well as someone to coordinate the delivery. Your client is likely to have strong personal taste in what they want, but will want you to track it down.

Likely Purchases

Appliances, sheets and bedding, vacuum cleaners, lamps, towels, storage units, window coverings.

General Tips

- These types of items are generally safe to purchase online, so long as your client is not in too much of a hurry. Most retailers have an online presence for this purpose.

- To track the latest trends in color and design for your clients, the International Home and Housewares Show is held every March in Chicago.

- Find out if clients have a preferred brand name that they associate with quality.

- Get as many details as possible in advance about how the product will be used to assist you in your selection. A vacuum for a small rug need not be the same type as one for wall-to-wall carpet.

Quick Links: Buying Housewares

- *Kitchen Appliance Selection Basics*
  http://interiordec.about.com/od/choosingappliances

- *HomeClick*
  www.homeclick.com

4. Getting Hired

Once you have developed your skills and knowledge of personal shopping, it's time to start getting paid for your talents.

As the title says, this chapter will help you get hired as a personal shopper for a particular business. If you would rather pursue starting your own personal shopping business, then you will find the advice you are looking for in chapter 5 (although you might still consider working for an employer first to get some hands-on experience).

We'll begin by taking a look at the types of industries that hire personal shoppers. Then we'll talk about how to find job openings, the materials you'll need for an interview, how to make a great impression on an interviewer and some great tips on how to get promoted out of an entry-level position. Throughout the chapter, you will receive advice from experts in the business about how to break into this fab job.

4.1 Types of Employers

4.1.1 Retail Industry

The retail industry offers some excellent career opportunities for personal shoppers. According to the experts, if you want a job in personal shopping, the best place to start is on a retail sales floor.

As mentioned in the Introduction, retail is far ahead of any other industry in terms of numbers of jobs for shoppers who want a steady paycheck. Retailing is one of the largest industries in the United States, and retail sales are forecast to remain solid in the near future, with annual growth increases predicted of six to nine percent.

Personal shopping is growing along with the industry. Once considered only for the rich, retailers are expanding and attempting to win over the middle class into this type of shopping as well. With more women in the workforce experiencing the challenges of balancing work and life, the need for personal shopping is growing in this sector.

Large High-End Retailers

Retailers in this category include Bergdorf Goodman, Bloomingdale's, Filene's, Holt Renfrew, Macys, Saks Fifth Avenue, and Tiffany & Co. You'll find links to major retailers who hire personal shoppers listed later in this chapter.

Local Boutiques

A boutique is a small retail shop that specializes in fashion, accessories or gifts. As someone who loves shopping, chances are you are already familiar with the top shopping districts and boutiques in your city.

Chicago, for example, has two very popular boutiques, Ikram and Ultimo. In New York, boutiques like Language and Scoop have personal shoppers. In the Los Angeles area the most famous location for boutiques is Rodeo Drive. There are many other boutiques in these cities and across the continent.

Specialty Retailers

Personal shoppers are hired by a variety of high-end retailers, in addition to those that sell gifts or apparel. For example, here is a recent job ad from toy retailer FAO Schwarz:

"We need a talented individual to fill the role of Personal Shopper for FAO Schwarz. In this commission-based position, you will be the one who serves customers; welcomes customers; directs customers; advises customers; provides information on products; helps customers make selections; offers suggestions; makes sales; documents sales; processes payments; keeps clientele informed of upcoming sales and future products."

Likewise, home furnishings companies (such as Ethan Allen and Thomasville) hire sales associates (sometimes called "designers") whose job involves selling the store's merchandise by helping customers choose products for their homes and businesses.

Shopping Centers

An increasing number of upscale shopping centers are hiring personal shoppers. Typically, these malls have high end retailers. For example, Americana Manhasset in Long Island, New York, has a personal shopper on staff to help clients find what they need at mall retailers such as Chanel, Hermès, and Ralph Lauren. The personal shopper at First Canadian Place in Toronto shops at mall retailers ranging from Baby Gap to Birks (Canada's top giftware store). Other malls, such as King of Prussia Mall in Pennsylvania, have online personal shoppers.

You can go online to see an example of the types of services offered in this position. Visit **www.americanaat manhasset.com** and click on "Personal Shopper."

4.1.2 Other Employers

As mentioned earlier in this guide, there are a variety of careers that involve shopping, although they are not exclusively personal shopping.

If you are interested in being a concierge (discussed in section 2.2), either as a career in itself or as a stepping-stone to a personal shopper position, you may find a variety of employers in your community. Concierges have been employed by hotels for many years. Concierges are also hired by upscale apartment complexes, gated communities, and real estate companies such as the nationwide firm Coldwell-Banker, and an increasing number of large corporations are providing concierge services for their employees.

4.2 Finding Job Openings

There are several places where jobs for personal shoppers may be advertised. If you're lucky, you may find a position in the classifieds of your local newspaper. However, most personal shopper jobs are not advertised in the classifieds, and it will take more effort to find job openings.

4.2.1 Advertised Positions

General Job Websites

Although there are no online job boards specializing in personal shopping, there are some general job sites that do post ads for personal shoppers. Plus many offer positions for sales associates. If a company hires sales associates, they might have personal shopper career opportunities. It's worth a phone call or e-mail to find out. Websites that sometimes have listings for personal shoppers include:

- *Careerbuilder*
  www.careerbuilder.com

- *HotJobs*
  www.hotjobs.com

- *Monster.com*
  www.monster.com

An excellent site to bookmark is on the About.com network. The site offers tips and advice, job boards and information about the retail industry. You can check it out at **http://retailindustry.about.com/library/blcareer.htm**.

Company Websites

Most companies advertise job openings on their websites. If there is no link for "jobs" or "careers" on the home page, click on the link for information about the company. That will usually take you to a page that includes a link to job postings.

Even if no positions are posted, many of these companies list store locations at their websites, and you could apply directly to the store or stores where you are interested in working. Here is a list of retailers that currently employ personal shoppers:

- *Barney's New York*
  www.barneys.com

- *Federated Department Stores*
  (Owns Bloomingdale's, Macy's, and several other stores)
  www.federated-fds.com

- *Holt Renfrew* (Canada)
  www.holtrenfrew.com/english

- *May Department Store Company*
  (Owns Filene's, Lord & Taylor and others)
  www.mayco.com

- *Neiman Marcus*
  www.neimanmarcus.com

- *Nordstrom*
  www.nordstrom.com

- *Saks Fifth Avenue*
  www.saksincorporated.com

- *Target Corporation*
  (Owns Marshall Field's)
  www.target.com

- *Tiffany & Co.*
  www.tiffany.com

There are a number of places to find links to other top companies in the United States and Canada. At Hoovers (**www.hoovers.com**), you can search for a specific company, or click on "Companies & Industries" to go to a page with a menu that allows you to browse a company directory or search by industries.

Fortune's list at **www.fortune.com/fortune/alllists** can provide you with information about the top companies in the U.S., while *Report on Business* has a list of the top companies in Canada at **www. globeinvestor. com/series/top1000**.

Types of Shopping Jobs

Following are some of the job titles you may hear when people talk about careers that involve shopping. You can search on all of these terms when looking for employment, but make sure you find out what the job entails, or you may find yourself disappointed with the lack of "shopping" you actually do.

Personal Shopper

Although the term personal shopper is used to describe people who consult with and shop for individual or corporate clients, some employers use this term to describe jobs that are customer service positions.

For example, when we first researched for this book, Jos. A. Bank Clothiers was advertising for full-time and part-time "personal shoppers." The positions were not in their retail stores, consulting with customers, but rather in their headquarters, taking telephone orders. There was certainly a component of consultation involved — the position required not only determining if what the customer wanted was in stock, but also advising on sizing and so on. While it isn't precisely personal shopping, it may be a way to get experience under your belt for a consultative personal shopping job.

Customer Service Specialist

Some retailers use this title for positions that involve personal shopping. Customer service specialist can mean other things, however. It can refer to a position in which you take care of customer complaints and problems, so be sure to ask exactly what the company means by the term before applying if you see it in an employment ad.

Gift Shopper

This term describes a personal shopper who specializes in buying gifts. It is sometimes used by gift stores.

Image Consultant

Many personal shoppers also do some "image consulting" – in other words, they give advice to clients about how to improve their appearance or wardrobe. If you work as a personal shopper in the apparel area of a retail store you will do image consulting as well as shopping.

Likewise, if you have your own personal shopping business, you will be an image consultant for clients who want you to buy clothing for them. However, the two careers are not exactly the same. Image consultants may give advice on many other aspects of appearance (e.g. hair and make-up), as well as behavior and communication skills – and they may not do any shopping for their clients.

Personal Concierge

This term is often used interchangeably with *personal shopper*, but as explained earlier, it really implies a greater range of services to a smaller clientele. If you are a personal concierge, you may take care of buying clothing, household goods, and gifts, but you will probably also do other day-to-day services for clients as well. It requires that you know a few customers, and their preferences and lifestyles extremely well.

Retail Consultant

This term is not used very often, and it often means just what it says: someone who consults with people planning purchases but does not actually do the shopping and buying. In fact, the term often refers to people who advise stores on a merchandise mix and so on. But you may hear the term, and it would be worth checking into if you see it in an employment advertisement.

Shopping Service Provider

This type of business is also known as an *errand and shopping service*. It is a form of personal shopping, but it involves shopping for precisely what the client asks for. The client will already have chosen an item, including the color, style, etc. and simply need you to pick it up for them.

In other words, much of the consultation aspect is removed from the duties. The items you pick up or shop for will be ordinary household goods, such as groceries, cleaning supplies, lawn care items and so on, and you will perform services such as picking up dry cleaning, prescriptions, and library books.

Stylist

Stylists specialize in fashion. They may offer image consulting and shopping services for celebrities (e.g. helping them pull together their look for an awards show), or they may be hired to do "styling" for photo shoots.

For example, they may select clothes for models in fashion magazines, find outfits for television shows, or coordinate the look of a group for a music video. While an element of shopping is involved with being a stylist, the more important skill is having a good eye for what will look good when photographed.

4.2.2 Unadvertised Positions

A study reported in the *Harvard Business Review* found that almost 80 percent of jobs are not advertised in the classifieds. That figure may be even higher for a fab job such as personal shopper. Susan Olden, vice president and director of Fifth Avenue Clubs for Saks Fifth Avenue says Saks – considered the pinnacle of personal shopping – typically doesn't advertise for personal shoppers, but rather uses word of mouth, existing employees (sales associates) and networking.

Even among the types of employers that usually do advertise for personal shoppers, smaller companies or boutiques may not have websites, and are unlikely to spend hundreds of dollars to post jobs at a site such as Monster.com. So how do these employers find employees?

Networking

Many employers find employees through word of mouth. When a small business owner needs a new employee, they will typically ask friends, business associates, and current employees if they know anyone who might be suitable for the job. In many cases, this is how they find the person for the job. Many human resources folks and other hiring managers "pass" resumes around.

If you can network with Employer A, who may not have an opening at any given time, you can impress them enough that they may be willing to pass your resume along to a company they know that is hiring. If you wish to get hired, you must get on as many radar screens as possible. As you've probably figured out by now, looking for a job is a job in itself!

In section 6.3.1 of this guide you will find practical advice on how to network to find personal shopping clients. You can also use the advice in this part of the guide to help you meet and connect with people who can hire you – or recommend you to someone who can hire you – for a full-time or part-time personal shopper position.

Direct Contact

Even if you don't know anyone connected to a particular company, it may still be possible to get a job there by contacting the company directly. It happens rarely, but sometimes a manager will have just decided that they need a new person, when they happen to receive a phone call or resume from someone who looks like they might be an ideal candidate for the job. Many employers would rather find someone this way than invest all the time and effort in advertising the job, screening resumes, and interviewing numerous candidates.

As mentioned in section 2.4.3, you can also try to schedule information interviews with professionals in the business and ask them for advice. Since someone is giving you precious time – and time is money in any business – don't push them to hire you, but rather keep in mind you're on a fact-finding mission. If the person you're networking with makes it clear that they have no openings at present, don't push it, because if they have a future opening and you impress them, you may get the call.

Other ideas can include making contact by telephone, email, or mail. If you decide to make "cold" contact with employers (as opposed to the "warm" contacts that come through networking), it's a good idea to focus on specific types of employers. This allows you to target your job search most effectively since it takes time to track down company owners' names, tailor your resume, and prepare personalized cover letters explaining why you want to work with that particular company.

See section 4.4.2 for more about cover letters, and section 6.4.2 for tips on how to track down contact information and make cold calls.

4.3 What Employers Are Looking For

Before preparing a resume or going on interviews, it helps to have a sense of what employers are looking for.

Chapter 2 described a number of general skills employers are looking for, including communication and sales skills. Here are some specific skills and experience sought by major retailers in recent advertisements seeking personal shoppers:

Macy's East

- A minimum of three years in retail management and in wardrobe selling

- A keen sense of fashion

- Superior selling skills

- Willingness to be a leader and team player

- Strong organizational, interpersonal and communication skills

- A strong client following

Nordstrom

For a telephone-based personal shopper position, Nordstrom Direct wanted...

- Six months sales experience

- Ability to develop rapport quickly and maintain good customer relationships

- Excellent follow-through and attention to detail

- Ability to work in a fast-paced environment and handle a high call volume

- Proven problem-solving skill coupled with the ability to remain solution-oriented at all times

- Exceptional conflict management skills and the ability to maintain a positive and professional composure

FAO Schwarz

- Encourages open communication by listening attentively and actively.

- Is a compelling and articulate speaker in a variety of settings. Easily adjusts the message to match the audience.

- Promotes excellence by providing superior service to each customer.

- Demonstrates talent at interacting effectively with all types of people.

- Inspires others with enthusiasm and positive energy.

- Demonstrates expert knowledge of the competitive market.

- Has a successful track record working with sales organizations to achieve and exceed their sales goals.

The more senior the position is, the more likely employers will look for someone with a client following. Of course, the specific skills employers are looking for may vary from one position to another, so carefully read the job advertisement and tailor your job-hunting materials to show the employer why you have exactly what they are looking for.

4.4 Job-Hunting Materials

Your resume and cover letter are important tools in helping you get the job you are looking for. In this section you will find advice for creating a resume and cover letter specifically for a personal shopper position. For general resume writing information visit Monster.com's Resume Center at **http://resume.monster.com**.

4.4.1 How to Prepare a Resume

Here is the good news: Even if you have never been paid to be a personal shopper, you can write a powerful resume that can help you secure a position as a personal shopper.

In order to do this you will need to get some personal shopping experience using several of the methods suggested in chapter 2. Even if the only shopping you've done is for friends and family members, you will still have shopping experience. The key is to present that experience in a way that demonstrates your value to employers and their clients.

Employers are most concerned with the value you will bring to them as an employee. They want to know you have the specific skills required to fulfill the duties and responsibilities of the position. They are not interested in reading about every previous job you have had if those jobs are unrelated to the one you're applying for.

Some employers make a decision about a resume within seconds, so a resume containing too much irrelevant information could be rejected before the employer has even finished reading it. Therefore, instead of submitting a traditional resume focusing on each job you held and what you did, create a functional resume focusing on the skills, experience and most importantly, the (hopefully positive) results of your experience.

Exactly what you will include on your resume depends on both the job you are applying for and your previous experience. You will find a sample resume in this section used to apply for a position working as a shopper for a high-end retailer. It assumes the person applying has some personal shopping experience for charities and friends, as well as previous retail experience.

Your own resume could include different categories. For example, if you are applying for a concierge job, it's a good idea to emphasize your organizational skills.

Other basic principles of preparing an effective resume are the same as for any job. For example, try to keep your resume to a single page unless you have extensive relevant experience. Also, you don't need to go back further than 10 years on your resume, since some employers may judge anything you learned before then to be outdated.

Sample Resume

Sharon Shopper

4321 Main Street
Sunnyday, California
(123) 555-1212
shopper@abc.com

Objective

To secure a position as a personal shopper utilizing my education, customer service and sales skills.

Personal Shopper

- Advised clients on: all matters to satisfy needs, clothing (child and adult), accessories and shoes
- Purchased best quality for clients while staying within their budgets with minimal returns
- Arranged and supervised selection of goods purchased
- Multi-tasking purchasing, selecting purchases for several clients concurrently
- Recognized for completing projects ahead of schedule and under budget

Customer Service and Sales Representative

- Used effective listening skills to determine customer needs and recommend products
- Kept in touch with customers by phone to ensure satisfaction and repeat sales
- Received letters of recommendation from satisfied clients (copies available on request)
- Consistently exceeded sales targets by more than 10 percent

Work and Volunteer Experience

- Self-employed Personal Shopper, Shop with Sharon, 2004
- Homemaker, 1997-2003
- Previous experience as a sales representative for several retail outlets including Lord & Taylor

Education

Successfully completed courses in Fashion Merchandising, Customer Service and Sales, Sunnyday College Continuing Education, 2003-2004

Something else to keep in mind is that you are applying for a job where appearance matters. Choose an attractive paper stock, lay it out nicely on the page, and make sure there are no typos. Ask someone else to look it over before you send it out.

4.4.2 Cover Letters

If you are submitting your resume by mail, fax or e-mail, include a cover letter. While it's okay to photocopy your resume, your cover letter should be personalized and should explain why you are a good candidate for the job. To see what to do – and what not to do – in a cover letter, here are some sample letters prepared in response to this ad for a personal shopper with a high-end retailer in New York City:

PERSONAL SHOPPER

As a personal shopper and corporate sales executive, you will work with individual customers and corporate clients to identify and satisfy their fashion and corporate requirements. Through direct customer selling and on-the-floor interaction, you will be responsible for growing your client base and setting the example for superior customer service. The ideal candidate will possess extensive sales experience, a keen sense of fashion, superior selling skills, as well as a client following. This is an entrepreneurial position with bottom line accountability to achieve sales goals.

Sample Letter 1

Dear Sirs:

I saw you're ad. This is the kind of job I've been looking for. I'm pretty sure I would enjoy it and it would be good experience for me. I've already sent out a bunch of resumes without much luck so I hope you'll hire me. As you can see I have everything your looking for. It's your loss if you don't hire me. Call me at 5555-1212.

Sharon Shopper

In the cover letter above, Sharon has done a number of things wrong. See how many of these mistakes you noticed:

Incorrect Salutation

Sharon could make a better impression by addressing the letter to the appropriate hiring manager by name. If you don't know who to send your letter to, you can access the company's website and look for the appropriate person. If this tactic is unsuccessful, you can call the personal shopping department at the particular retailer and ask whom the appropriate manager is, then address your letter to that person.

Even if the advertisement reads "send letters to human resources," don't address the letter to "Human Resources." In most cases, the human resources department screens applicants, so go directly to the source. Send it to the decision maker because, nine times out of ten, the decision maker is going to be the person you would eventually work for if you get hired. The worst thing that can happen is that the manager of the personal shopping department will forward your materials up to human resources. It's worth a shot.

If there is no other way but to address your letter to human resources and you don't know the gender of the person you're sending the letter to, then avoid gender salutations such as "Dear Sirs," and rather write "Dear Sir or Madam."

What's the Position?

The letter doesn't state what position Sharon is applying for. Many companies advertise more than one position at a time. Omitting the position demonstrates lack of attention to details.

Typographical and Grammatical Errors

Letters must be proofread before being sent. You'll never hear a compliment on an error-free resume or cover letter; they're supposed to be perfect. While there's no correlation between good spelling and intelligence, nothing turns off a prospective employer more than a sloppy resume. The attitude is that a sloppy resume equals an employee that doesn't pay attention to details.

Furthermore, don't rely too heavily on your word processor's spell check since it won't catch mistakes such as using "two" instead of "too." Ask a friend to read the letter for you — the most difficult part of proofreading anything is catching your own mistakes.

Failing to Address the Company's Needs

Sample Letter 1 doesn't address the company's needs that are clearly written in the advertisement. Sharon writes that she wants to "enjoy the job and get experience," instead of directly addressing what the company wants. Employers want to know what value you will bring to them.

You should focus on what the results of your efforts were (such as sales figures or client base), not a rehash of a job description. Anyone can sell clothes; it's the expert and the one who can bring the company a customer for life that will ultimately get hired.

Failing to Mention the Company by Name

Sharon could make a much better impression by doing a little research in order to say something flattering about the company. You can find out what a company prides itself on by checking its website. The best place to start would be in the "About Us" section of the site.

Negativity

By stating, "I've already sent out a bunch of resumes without much luck," and "I hope you'll hire me," Sharon sounds desperate. Employers may wonder if there's a good reason why no one else has hired her. And as you can imagine, writing something like, "It's your loss if you don't hire me" does not make a good impression.

If you were an employer, wouldn't you be more impressed with Sample Letter 2 on page 95? It explains what Sharon has done and what she can do for ABC Incorporated. Your own cover letter will of course depend on the position you are applying for, and the company you are applying to. It should also include your contact information at the top of the page.

4.4.3 Letters of Recommendation

The best letters of recommendation are those written by people you have shopped for. However, you can also include letters of recommendation from past employers, if the letters say good things about your abilities in areas that are important as a shopper, such as interpersonal skills and organizational ability. Recent college graduates can also ask for letters from instructors. You can also include any appropriate thank-you notes you have received.

Sample Letter 2

Ms. Jane Doe
Vice President, Personal Shopping Division
ABC Incorporated

Dear Ms. Doe:

In response to your [Day, Month, Date] advertisement in the Tribune, I'm writing this letter to offer myself as a candidate for the position of personal shopper with ABC Incorporated.

Having read the mission statement on your corporate web page, I find that our professional personalities and goals for service, dedication and excellence are closely aligned.

As you will see in my resume, I have previous experience as a personal shopper with an established client base that I've grown since my tenure with XYZ Corporation. In fact, I've grown my sales 60 percent over the past two years. I offer these skills to ABC Incorporated.

My experience, education in Fashion Merchandising and existing customer base makes a strong recipe for success with ABC Incorporated. I excel at customer service, have a keen fashion sense, work hard to get repeat business for my employer, and have numerous letters of recommendation from satisfied customers and clients.

I would be thrilled to meet with you or one of your associates to discuss my candidacy for personal shopper with ABC Incorporated at your earliest possible convenience.

Thank you and I look forward to hearing from you soon.

Best,
Sharon Shopper

As was emphasized in section 2.4.4, every time you do shop for some-one – even a friend or family member (with a different last name from yours) – ask for a letter of recommendation. Recommendation letters look particularly impressive if they are on letterhead, so ask for several copies on letterhead if possible.

> **TIP:** A recommendation letter should preferably not mention if you worked for free. You want to demonstrate that your work has value, and an employer may assume the reason you received a glowing recommendation is because you didn't charge any-thing. Remember, good work is good work no matter how much you were paid for it.

When you ask for a letter, keep in mind that many people are busy, so they are more likely to do what you ask if you can make it as easy as possible. To help get the kind of recommendation letter you want, and make the job easier on the person writing the letter, you could supply a list of points they might mention. For example:

- The specific work you performed on their behalf (write it out for them – chances are you remember what you did more clearly than they might)

- Your exceptional knowledge of products or trends

- You got the shopping done ahead of schedule

- You regularly reminded them of special gift-giving occasions they might otherwise have forgotten

- You had excellent recommendations for products within their bud-get

- You came up with many creative ideas

- You listened and delivered exactly what they wanted

- People have commented on how beautifully dressed your client was

Of course, all these things don't have to be included in a single letter. The specifics will depend on the particular job you did, but even a few glowing sentences can help you look good to employers.

Portfolio

Another way to demonstrate your expertise is with a portfolio. Your portfolio could include "before" and "after" pictures of your clients. It can also include other items that show your skills. For example, if you won a sales award, put the actual certificate or award in your portfolio. If that's not possible, include photocopies or a photograph of the award.

Likewise, if you wrote an article relevant to personal shopping that was published in a newspaper or magazine, you could include a clipping or photocopy of the published article. See section 6.3.4 for information about how to write articles for publication, and other ways to establish your reputation as a personal shopping expert. See section 6.2.2 for more information about how to create a portfolio.

4.5 Interviews

Interviews for personal shopping positions are similar to interviews for other jobs. With that in mind, there are several specific tips that can help make an excellent impression in an interview.

4.5.1 What Employers Expect

These days, retail is all about "repeat customers," or as Arthur Martinez, former chairman, president and CEO of Sears, Roebuck and Co. used to say, "a customer for life." Of course employers are looking for someone who will do an excellent job, but they are also seeking someone with certain character and personality traits.

Attitude

> "A candidate's personality must be up and happy and we want people who have a true passion for the business. If a candidate can't woo me, they can't woo our clients."
>
> — *Susan Olden, Saks Fifth Avenue*

Your attitude is being evaluated from the moment you first walk into the building, or even earlier, when you first speak on the telephone with anyone from the company. Anyone you encounter in the parking lot, the elevator, the washroom, or the reception area may have input into whether or not you are hired. Some interviewers have asked the receptionist what they thought of the person. Companies want to know an applicant will treat everyone with respect, not just the interviewer.

During the interview itself, try to be as outgoing and enthusiastic as possible. This isn't always easy because interviews can make people nervous, and nervous people tend to smile less, and act more stiff and formal than they normally would. However, as a personal shopper, you will be working with many people, including clients. The employer wants to see that you are comfortable even in a potentially uncomfortable interpersonal situation such as an interview.

If you tend to be stiff and uncomfortable during an interview, it is time to perform. Act how you would if you did not feel nervous. This may feel unnatural at first, but behaving as if you are not nervous can actually make you start to feel that way as well. It can also help to do some roleplaying (practice interviews) with a friend before you go to the interview.

As well as being enthusiastic, be positive. Avoid saying anything negative, especially about former employers. Focus on what value you would bring to the company as an employee, and not on what you want to get from the job. For example, don't discuss how much vacation time you want or bring up salary until the employer does.

Also avoid saying anything negative about yourself, which some applicants do by sounding as if they are desperate for a job. Before the interview, remind yourself how much you have to offer an employer, and that there are many opportunities for you. Believe that if this particular job doesn't work out, there is something better out there for you.

Above all, you want the interviewer and the other people you meet to think: "What a nice person! It would be great to have someone like that working here."

4.5.2 How to Dress

Personal shopping is a visual business, so it's not surprising that you'll be judged by your appearance more than in other careers.

Barbara Moses, Ph.D., author of the best-selling book *Career Intelligence*, advises applicants to think about what the interviewer might be wearing, and to match the style:

> "Effective presentation as a job candidate means showing that you understand the culture in which you would be operating and that you would readily fit in."

Susan Olden adds:

> "Our personal shoppers have to fit the 'Saks Look.' They must be very well-groomed, neat, nothing over done. We want them to look 'middle ground.'"

Here are some specific tips for men and women on how to dress for interviews:

Men

If you're a man, dressing up is a bit more challenging since you are limited to the basic shirt, slacks, tie, etc. So use the advantages of color, pattern and styles to compensate.

Suits

It's always better to wear a suit (a three button jacket is always nice) to an interview rather than a jacket-slack combination since you want to look as professional as possible. Make sure you're color-specific to the current season. It's essential to be comfortable, so don't wear a wool suit – no matter how good it looks – in summer!

Olden says label make no difference to her. She's just as impressed with a suit from Lord & Taylor as from Hugo Boss. The key is, whatever you wear, make sure it makes you look good.

Shirts

Nothing beats a nice, clean, starchy white cotton shirt, but that doesn't mean you can't jazz up your look. For example, if you're wearing a navy blue suit with gray pinstripes, then choose a shirt that matches the color of the pinstripe to bring it out. Further, mixing and matching different patterns of ties and shirts is excellent as well.

If you're a smaller man and have trouble with dress shirts that have too much material, Olden suggests having a few custom-made dress shirts in your wardrobe. It's more expensive but well worth the money.

Ties

When it comes to ties, make sure they're not too wide or thin. If you don't know how to tie a fancy knot, there are many web sites that actually have tips for tie tying, such as **www.tieanecktie.com/index.php**.

Shoes

First and foremost, make sure your shoes are shined! Nothing will dress you up like a nice shiny pair of shoes; nothing will make you look more slovenly than a dirty, scuffed pair. Unkempt shoes denote a lack of detail. As far as style, leather is good, wingtips are ultra-conservative and a can't-miss.

Accessories

Olden loves suspenders. You can mix and match your suspenders, tie and shirts, or go all out and buy sets. Also, cufflinks are a great addition to any man's closet.

Women

Olden tells us that she likes to see women who are somewhere in the middle — not too conservative but nothing overdone.

Suits

Suits are a great look for personal shoppers — sleek and professional with a wide variety to choose from. The only thing to be mindful of is the hemlines. Make sure they're not too short, but you can go as long as you like.

Shirts and Blouses

Most materials will work, from cotton to satin. The key here is to avoid plunging neck-lines and don't wear blouses that are overly fitted.

Shoes

Olden says she likes to see a variety of shoe types. Mid-height heels are fine, but keep them under three inches. Olden also stresses that your shoes MUST match your outfit. Make sure your shoes are clean, and shine them if necessary.

Dresses

There's nothing wrong with a dress. But again, be mindful of the hem-line and neck line. Also make sure to pick a style and pattern that fits your body type. Horizontal stripes on a short, medium-bodied woman will not work.

Accessories

It's not advisable to carry both a handbag and a briefcase to the inter-view. If you absolutely need certain items in your purse, then select only what you need, put it in a small make-up bag and tuck it out of sight in your briefcase. Black or brown are great colors for bags since they go with everything. Keep jewelry simple and elegant. This is something Olden looks for — trendy is OK, just nothing over the top.

Hairstyles

Olden says pink hair standing straight up will not impress her. On the other hand, she likes to see variety combined with style, imagination and taste. Here, the key is to make sure the interviewer can clearly see your face, so keep the bangs out of your eyes. If you wear long hair, put it up in a French braid, bun or weave. If you color your hair, make it look natural.

Make-up

You're going to a job interview, not a date. So make yourself look the part. Minimally, some blush, eye shadow and a nice lip gloss are in order. You can match your lip gloss to your outfit to really show your sense of style and attention to detail. She also advises to be selective with perfume; an overpowering scent, no matter how pleasant, will distract the interviewer.

Other Advice

> **TIP:** Travel around to several stores that employ personal shoppers and get an idea of what they wear and how they wear it.

If you have no information to go on, choose standard interview attire, such as a navy suit, but with a subtle twist. Use your clothing to show that you are creative and have a good eye. A man might wear a tie with an interesting pattern while a woman might wear an accessory such as an unusual pin or another striking piece of jewelry. Whatever you choose should say something about you and your style.

4.5.3 Interview Questions

In most interviews, you can expect to be asked questions such as those in the following list. It's a good idea to prepare some answers to these questions before the interview. It's also a good idea to roleplay an interview with a friend so your answers will come naturally.

- Why do you want to work for our company?

- What drew you to a career in personal shopping?

- What kind of position are you looking for?

- What did you like most about your last job? What did you like least? Why?

- What experience do you have with _____? (Depending on the company, they may want to know your experience with personal shopping, sales numbers, customer service, working in teams, juggling many projects at once, etc.)

- What are your strengths? What are your weaknesses?

- Where do you see yourself in five years?

- What are your salary expectations?

- Do you have any questions for us?

You can find some more advice on preparing for an interview and answering standard interview questions from Monster.com's Interview Center at **http://interview.monster.com**.

In order to ask good questions and give an effective answer to the question "Why do you want to work here?" you will need to learn something positive about the company prior to the interview. Visit and read the company's website, if they have one, or stop by the office to pick up any promotional brochures. Reading the company's press releases is also a good indicator of what the company is up to.

Sample Answers

When the interviewer asks you "Why do you want to work for this company?" you can pick out the best things about the company and relate them to your own goals. For example, you might say, "When I found out you made home deliveries as early as 1898, I was impressed. With service like that, I would have been a loyal customer. I think the store still has that attitude, and I would love to be a part of it."

When the interviewer asks "Where do you see yourself in five years?" a good answer might be: "I want to have a client list that keeps me busy and challenges me to give them the best this store has to offer."

Another good answer might be: "I would like to be in a management position so I can help us get started on another hundred years of being the best store in the Midwest." (A bad answer would be: "Living on the Riviera with a rich boyfriend." Make sure your answer relates to your job.)

If the interviewer asks you to "Tell me a little about yourself," pick the highlights of your abilities and your career, and enthusiastically use 60 seconds or so to tell the interviewer those things. The interviewer will likely then ask you about your strengths and weaknesses. Don't be negative, but don't be pompous, either. Accentuate the positive and play down the negative.

For example, you know you tend to talk a little too much; on the other hand, you know that what you say usually interests people. So say, "I can talk with just about anyone about just about anything very easily, and I use that ability to put people at ease." That also tells the interviewer you are a "people person," a very important attribute for a personal shopper.

Also be prepared to answer behavioral questions. These are questions that ask you about an experience you had in the past, and require you to answer with a specific real-life example. The interviewer might ask: "Tell me about a time you had to deal with a difficult customer. What happened, and how was it resolved?"

The interviewer will not be satisfied with a hypothetical answer about what you "would" do in such a situation. They want to hear about an actual time you experienced conflict with a customer. The purpose is not to see if you have ever had a conflict (they expect you have). The purpose is to see how well you resolve difficult situations and, if something did not work out in the past, what you learned from it.

Aside from the standard questions, Olden says she asks questions that don't relate exactly to the position, but rather tries to get a feel for the candidate's style and tastes. "I look for the intangibles. For example, you can't teach someone 'appropriateness,' or basic good manners," she says.

Other Tips

Try to build rapport with the interviewer. It could mean the difference between them hiring you or hiring another, equally qualified, applicant.

When you enter the interviewer's space, look for something that interests you and that you can ask about intelligently. For example, if the interviewer is playing Celtic music in the background, ask about it. Showing sincere interest in something that's meaningful to the interviewer will help build rapport.

Also, how you conduct yourself when you don't know how to answer will affect whether you are hired or not. If you need time to think of an answer, repeat the question or rephrase it. That will indicate that you are a thoughtful person, not one who blurts things out without thinking.

4.5.4 Discussing Salary

If an employer is interested in hiring you, they will bring up the issue of salary. You should not be the first one to bring up salary if you want to make a good impression on the interviewer.

If you are applying for an existing position then the human resources and personal shopping departments will already have budgeted a specific salary range for the position. If you are the first one to mention a specific salary figure, and it's lower than the one the employer had in mind, you risk getting hired for less than they might have been willing to pay you.

Therefore, if they ask your salary expectations, give them an open-ended answer such as, "I would expect a salary that matches my current level of education, skill and prior work experience. What is the salary range for this position?"

In many cases, you may be able to negotiate a better salary or better benefits than the employer's initial offer. If the employer isn't flexible on salary, they may be able to offer higher commissions, or be willing to negotiate vacation or overtime. At this stage you can also discuss preferred working hours (many clients will want to meet with you either at lunch or very early or very late in the day).

The typical base salary for a retail sales associate in New York, Chicago and Los Angeles is between $24,000-$25,000 per year. Of course, the figures above are for standard sales jobs. A personal shopper working on salary or a combination of base pay and commissions can earn in the mid-$30,000 figures their first year. And that amount can easily go up from there, especially as the shopper's client base grows. Plus, in addition to a base salary and commission, shoppers working for retailers may also earn substantial discounts on merchandise.

The difference in salary really depends on the position you apply for. Your position may be considered a sales position, or a marketing position, or even a managerial position. You may report to other supervisors, or you may supervise other employees.

If the position is for a large department store, you will specialize in specific areas; if it's a smaller business, you may have to do it all. All of these factors above can affect your salary, and it's a good idea to ask questions about things like this during your interview. It's also a good idea to have a sense of how much you should be getting paid before the issue comes up during an interview. In retail, it's typical that an employee will get a draw against commission. Since there's no way to measure how much any one person will sell, the earnings potential are limitless.

To get information about typical salaries in your community, connect with people in the retail industry using the techniques described in this guide, such as informational interviews (see section 2.4.3), mentoring, and networking (see section 6.3.1). You can also find average salaries for sales or retail positions at **www.salary.com**.

While effective negotiations can lead to a higher salary, if you really want an unlimited potential for income, then you should consider being self-employed. In the next chapter you will learn how to start your own personal shopping business.

4.5.5 Following Up

Following up after an interview can be as important as the interview itself. Within 24 hours after the interview, follow up with a thank-you letter or e-mail to the person or persons you interviewed with. Your thank-you note should achieve three things:

- Thank the interviewer for their time

- State whether you do or do not wish to continue the interview process

- Make one final sales pitch as to why you're the right person for the position

You can use your computer's software to make personal letterhead with your name and contact information.

Sample Thank-You Note

Ms. Jane Doe
Director, Personal Shopping Division
ABC Company

Dear Ms. Doe:

I just wanted to take a moment to thank you for taking time from your busy schedule to meet with me today to discuss my candidacy for personal shopper with ABC Company and to tell you that I'd be thrilled to continue the interviewing process.

I feel my current level of education, experience and existing client base is a great match with your company's current personal shopping needs.

Remembering during our discussion that it's part of your company's current operating business plan to increase your personal shopper client base by five percent by the end of your current fiscal year, my existing client base would greatly assist in attaining that goal.

If you require any additional information, please do not hesitate to contact me by either phone or e-mail.

Thank you and I look forward to hearing from you soon.

Best,

Sharon Shopper

4.6 Success on the Job

4.6.1 Getting Promoted from an Entry-Level Job

Congratulations! You have that first job, and in the personal shopping business, if you're working for a retailer, the first place you'll begin this exciting fab job is on the sales floor. Now that you're there, here are some tips on getting that promotion.

Know Your Company's Promotion Guidelines

If you're working for a big box retailer or national chain, the company will have written requirements for promotions. Usually it comes down to a set amount of time in your current position or division. For example, Sears requires employees to stay in their current position for one 18-month business cycle.

Become a Student of the Game

It's not enough just to know how to sell or service your clients and customers. If you want to get ahead, you have to understand how retailing works. If your department suddenly goes through a retro refit, then find out why. Nothing happens on a retail sales floor by chance — if your department is getting a refit then it's the result of hours of meetings, studies, focus groups and marketing techniques by upper management.

If you have a degree in fashion merchandising or something similar, you have a step over the competition as to why things happen. If you don't have a degree, then you'll have to ask questions. It's the employee who understands why and how things work that gets promoted the quickest.

Take Initiative

With companies downsizing like crazy, there are fewer employees to do the same work but they are still expected to keep performance and sales levels up.

The employee who needs the least amount of supervision will be the one who gets noticed. Don't wait for someone to ask you to do something you know is required. If the department you work in is messy and you're not with a customer, then clean it up before you're asked. Show that you take your own initiative and need minimal supervision and you'll endear yourself to your superiors.

Get a Mentor

Every Anakin has an Obi-Wan. Your mentor could be your supervisor, a former college professor, or a fellow co-worker with more experience than yourself. Your mentor is the person you want to be like. Find that person, ask them questions, and learn all you can from them — there's no substitute for that experience.

Work on Leadership Skills

Some leaders are made, and some are born. Either way, being an effective leader takes training and skill. Learn the difference between being the boss and being bossy.

If your company offers classes or training in leadership, take them. Another possibility is to take classes or seminars on your own. While corporate budgets are always stretched, ask your supervisor if the company would be willing to pick up the cost. Even if they say no, your sales manager will probably be impressed with your drive.

Keep Returns to a Minimum

All too often, sales associates only concentrate on the sale at hand. If you oversell your customer then they'll suffer from buyer's remorse and most likely will return the item. Retail sales are all about numbers. Be assured that your employer will know every product sold — and every product returned.

While sales are important, the current theme in retailing is repeat business. Sell the customer only what they want and need — no more. If you impress them, chances are they'll be back and you'll have a "customer for life."

Go Above and Beyond the Call of Duty

Employers want to know you're the type of person who will do what is necessary to get the job done. A very popular interview question is, "Tell me about a time that you went above and beyond the call of duty for your employer." Above and beyond can include anything, from volunteering for extra shifts, to creative thinking on a customer's problem, to a new idea on how to improve communication between departments. Another way to go above and beyond is by using creative promotional tactics.

4.6.2 Effective Marketing and Promotion

You will often be expected to attract new clients to the personal shopper service. If you work for a major retailer, you will get promotional help from your marketing and advertising departments. But you will still have to use your head to promote both your service and the goods you sell. Your personality and attention to their needs are two factors that will retain your clients. But you will also need to keep track of promotional efforts you make.

Your employer will expect many of these tactics, and you will be provided with the means to accomplish them. But not all employers will provide for all of them. To be a stunning success, do on your own those tactics your employer doesn't expect or provide for. Here are promotional tactics that will set you apart from others:

Mailing List

You will have the names, addresses and e-mail addresses of everyone you serve. As you collect that information for billing purposes, also transfer it to a paper- or computer-based database you can use to send out such things as sale reminder notices.

Sale Reminder Notices

Encourage customers to use the sale as a starting point for a wardrobe or room décor checkup and so on. Sometimes sales occur at the beginning of a season when you might be busy anyway. But they can also be planned to attract customers during slow periods. Use your mailer to offer extra attention or services you have time for now.

Community Service

Your clients are, almost by definition, already too busy. So you wouldn't benefit by asking them to help you plant trees on Earth Day. But you could benefit by asking them to sponsor a walk for some organization. Send them a letter with a return envelope asking them to sponsor a certain number of miles; they return their donation in the envelope. And after you've completed the walk, send them a photo of yourself on the walk in a nice thank-you card. You are in a business that depends on goodwill, and that's sometimes more important than specific merchandise you sell.

Events

You may have the leeway to plan events for your customer list. These can be as simple as an afternoon tea on a Saturday featuring a drawing for a free facial and a short talk by the store's salon manager. Or they can be as elaborate as a designer trunk show or fashion show with runway models.

Schedule events frequently, knowing that not all your customers will be able to make it to all of them. And some customers won't ever make it; after all, they hire a personal shopper to save shopping time. But they do like being asked.

Charity Tie-ins

Here's a chance to use your negotiating skills. Perhaps you can convince one of your most popular vendors to make a charitable donation for every item bought by your clients in a particular month. You can use that information in your mailer to influence new purchases and promote your generosity and that of your vendors. Many customers will respond positively to that, and become more loyal than they might otherwise be.

Go Out and Meet People

Networking groups are great for personal shoppers. At many of them, you can hand out your card, and every so often the floor will be yours for the meeting.

Naturally, anyone you help in the group becomes another walking advertisement for you. This sort of promotion is priceless. It costs very little,
takes very little time – you have to eat anyway, and they are usually
breakfast or lunch meetings – and can pay off in a big way. You might
even meet some new friends.

Better yet, you might even find a new vendor to add to those from whom
you get the interesting, unique products that help make you so valuable
to the shopping-impaired.

Contests

Use your creativity to develop a couple of contests each year. People
love to win, or at least feel like they might be able to win. It is a positive
way to get your services into their "top of mind" awareness again. It may
not result in more sales that day, but over time, the effect of all you do to
keep your name in front of customers adds up.

For example, have a professor from a local university that offers fashion
design pick a winner of a "before and after" contest featuring snapshots
of your clients before and after you helped them with their wardrobe. If
you're specializing in gift items, make it a letter about "the greatest thank
you" your client ever got for a gift you helped with, judged by a local
celebrity. And, of course, award a meaningful prize.

Life Event Greetings

Read your local community news. When you see that one of your customers has won a civic award, or that her son has gotten married, or
that her daughter has been accepted to Harvard…whatever happy event
occurs, send an appropriate card.

Birthdays, of course, are a given; you will collect that information anyway
when you create your customer files. And you may also be faced with
sending a card on a sad occasion, such as a death in the family. Don't
avoid those, especially if it concerns a frequent or major client, or one
with whom you have built a particularly good relationship. These cards
are certainly more difficult to send than happy cards, but they are appreciated.

4.6.3 A Personal Shopper Success Story

Many experts offered their tips and advice for this chapter on getting hired as a personal shopper. We now close the chapter with an inspiring story of one personal shopper's success.

You could say for Rosina Constantino, fashion is in her blood.

The daughter of a men's clothing manufacturer (her dad, who she says was a great inspiration in her life), this New Yorker, who graduated in 1979 from a prestigious New York City university with a major in Fashion Merchandising, has been in the business for 24 years and is currently a consultant with Saks Fifth Avenue's Fifth Avenue Club.

Her beginnings were much more humble, though. Costantino answered an advertisement in the *New York Times* and was hired as a personal shopper's assistant with a major New York retailer shortly after she graduated from college. Rosina excelled so well as an assistant that she was promoted to sales associate within eight short months.

She climbed quickly because her sales numbers were astronomical. Additionally, she found a mentor as a personal shopping assistant and learned everything she could from her. She paid attention to the little things and offered customers a pleasant shopping experience. She also read everything she could get her hands on, from *The Wall Street Journal* to *Vogue*, in order to keep up with fashion and business.

She stayed with her first employer for six years. After three more retailers and a solid core of clients behind her, she got the call from Saks in 1992. Costantino got that call because she spent her entire career learning the business and making contacts. As it happened, one of her clients had a contact at Saks.

Costantino's contact suggested her to Saks, and that led her to the position that, as this book was first being researched, she had held for more than 10 years.

Costantino suggests that beginners remember the human factor of the business. Step number one, she says, is to always remember that the customer is not an interruption to your workday but rather, the one and only reason you're there.

Relationships are also important — relationships with co-workers, other departments, other professionals in the field and, of course, the clients.

Costantino remembers one occasion when she went to the Plaza Hotel in Manhattan to meet with a Saudi Arabian princess. After a short informational meeting, the princess hired Costantino and they arrived together at Saks at 4:00 p.m. — and she served her client until 1:00 a.m. Costantino said it's going the extra mile that has made her income grow some 400 percent since she's been in the business.

Costantino plans to keep up her business as long as her legs hold out. As a final piece of advice, she says, "If you have passion for the business and love what you do, personal shopping will come naturally to you."

5. Starting Your Own Business

Having a job shopping and advising others about what to buy seems just about perfect. Just about. But you're wondering if anything that good couldn't be just a tiny bit better. It's freedom you crave, and you'll grant that having a job as a personal shopper is about as free as it gets. Flexible hours, great working conditions, good pay, lots of interaction with lots of interesting people — it doesn't get any better than that, does it?

It can, if you're one of those people who not only likes to shop and help people, but who has wanted to be your own boss as well. As a personal shopper, the world, as they say, is your oyster. Or your Armani suit. Or your designer furniture. Or whatever you decide is the perfect niche for you in your community.

The information in this chapter will give you resources and information to start your own business. In the next chapter, you'll discover how to find and work with clients.

5.1 Getting Started

Before you can get to the fun part of having your own personal shopping business, there are a number of not so fun, but very important, matters to be handled. Here are the details of what needs to be done so you can prepare for a successful business.

5.1.1 Creating a Business Plan

Business planning involves putting on paper all the plans you have for your business, including:

- The services you will provide

- Where you will locate your business

- Who your clients are

- Who your competitors are

- Where you will find vendors of products and services

- What you will charge for your services

- How you will advertise and market your services

- How much money you will need to get started

After reading this chapter, and the next chapter on finding clients, you will be able to start creating your own business plan. It is a document you will probably read again and again as you start to operate your business.

The very first and last pages of your business plan should state your mission. It should be a simple statement, one you can remember even without looking at your plan. Keeping your mission in the forefront of your mind is a sure way of getting to your goal and having fun doing it.

Remember, too, that your business plan will help you decide the right time to start your business. It will help you decide if you have enough funds set aside to support yourself while it gets up and running.

While it has certainly happened, you can't count on getting your well-paying, quick-paying, repeat client the very first week!

Because it will take some time and some investigation to create your business plan, you may learn things that change your thoughts about how you will set up your business.

> **EXAMPLE:** You may have been planning to just shop for men's clothing and accessories. But you find that most of the businesses in your area are industrial, and the number of men who need to dress in suits and blazers to go to work is too small to support what you want to do. What then? Either branch out into women's clothing as well, or expand the geographical territory you are willing to serve until you find a population of executives large enough to support your services. Or, you may find any number of other creative ideas to do what you want – and be successful at it – in any business locale.

An excellent resource to help you come up with a business plan is available through the Small Business Administration. Visit their website at **www.sba.gov/starting_business/planning/basic.html**. American Express has helpful information on preparing a business plan at **www133. americanexpress.com/osbn/Tool/biz_plan/**.

5.1.2 Choosing a Business Name

Your business name needs to do several things. It must:

- Describe what you do

- Be easy to pronounce

- Attract customers

- Be unique

- Be available

Housewares/Electronics Shopping Service might describe what you do, and it's easy to pronounce, but it's boring, which doesn't help attract customers.

Your business name is the place to begin using your creativity and re-search skills. You might begin by finding out what the local department stores call their services. For example, Macy's calls theirs By Appointment. That wouldn't work for you, though, because people would ask themselves, "*What* by appointment?" And they won't call you to find out the answer. If you happen to use it as part of another name, such as Professional Image By Appointment, make sure you check the trademark offices (see below) to see that you can use it that way.

Names can be straightforward, like Professional Image By Appointment, or they might be more whimsical. An example is Silk Purse Shopping and Image Company, borrowing on the old idea of turning a sow's ear into a silk purse. But wait! If your potential clients know that phrase, they won't want to think of themselves as a sow's ear, even before you get hold of them. So choosing a good name involves more than just thinking up something clever.

Personal shopper Ilene Mackler calls her business Power Presents, and it works for her. But if you came upon it in the Yellow Pages, you might read it two ways. "Presents" can mean gifts, but the same spelling of the word can be a verb meaning "to exhibit or display," as in "She presents herself well." In that case, the company could be mistaken for an executive coaching firm.

When you've decided on a few names that meet all the specs, let some friends and colleagues know what you're thinking of calling your business, and ask for their comments and opinions. The decision is still up to you, of course, but the instant reactions of "real people" can be a good indication of whether you are on the right track or not.

In most jurisdictions, if you operate under anything other than your own name, you are required to file for a fictitious name. It's usually just a short form to fill out and a small filing fee that you pay to your state or provincial government. You can find links to the appropriate government departments for filing your name at **www.sba.gov/hotlist/businessnames.html**.

Before registering a fictitious name, you will need to make sure it doesn't belong to anyone else. You certainly wouldn't want to spend all your initial investment money, only to find out you couldn't legally operate under a name you had chosen because someone else owns the trademark.

So do some research on the names you like. You can do an online search of the federal trademark database to determine whether a name has already been registered.

For good advice on trademarks and other matters to consider before choosing a business name, check out Nolo.com's Small Business Resources at **www.nolo.com**. You will have to click on the "Business and Human Resources" tab; then "Starting a Business"; then "Naming Your Business" to view the relevant information.

Most start-up businesses do not bother to trademark their names because it can be costly and time-consuming. However, if your company name is truly unique, you might want to consider it. You can try doing it yourself, or hire a lawyer to do it for you.

5.1.3 Legal Matters

Your Business Legal Structure

A business can take several different legal forms. Which one you choose will have an impact on how much it costs to start and run your business. The sole proprietorship is the least costly way to go into business, but it doesn't afford some of the legal protections of a corporate structure. Here are the characteristics and benefits of various legal forms a business may take.

Sole Proprietorship

If you want to run the business yourself, without incorporating, your business will be known as a "sole proprietorship." This is the least expensive way to start your own business. It is also the easiest because it requires less paperwork and you can report your business income on your personal tax return. One drawback to this type of business is that you are personally liable for any debts of the business.

Partnership

If you want to start your shopping business with someone else, the easiest and least expensive way to do this is by forming a partnership. Legally, you would both be responsible for any debts of the company.

Working With a Partner

A good partnership requires a bit of planning if it is to run smoothly. You may want to have an attorney set up a legal partnership, spelling out what each partner contributes to and takes out of the business. Whether or not you form a legal partnership, talk with your partner and come to some firm conclusions about:

- What tasks each of you will be responsible for

- How you will make day-to-day business decisions, and how you will break a tie

- What percentage of the business each will own

- How you want the business to grow in the future

- What expectations you have of each other

It is better to find out the areas where you need to compromise before you open the doors. For example, you may want to work only on weekdays, but your partner prefers weekends and evenings. But what about when you need to meet to discuss issues in the business? And how will you deal with it if a client you have been serving suddenly decides evening meetings are best for him?

And what if a disproportionate number of clients prefer your hours, or your partner's, leaving one of you with the lion's share of the work? Will you divide the income to reflect that, or will you find ways to even out the workload and still have each partner serve the clients who prefer them? Another very important thing to consider is what to do if one partner decides to leave the business. Does the remaining partner take on all the clients, or approve a replacement?

Keep a list of the compromises you will make. When you have agreed upon all points, put them into a written "partnership agreement" signed by both of you.

Corporation

Whether you are working alone or with partners, if you want a more formal legal structure for your business, you can incorporate. Incorporation can protect you from personal liability and may make your business appear more professional to some clients.

However, it usually costs several hundred dollars and there are many rules and regulations involved with this type of business structure (among other requirements, corporations must file articles of incorporation, hold regular meetings, and keep records of those meetings). Many new business owners consult with an attorney before incorporating.

Limited Liability Company

A Limited Liability Company is a newer type of business legal structure in the U.S. It is a combination of a partnership and corporation, and is considered to have some of the best attributes of both, including limited personal liability.

Business Licenses

If you are planning to sell wholesale items, you will need a business license as well as a resale number (covered in secion 3.2). Call your city hall to get the location of your local Occupational License Office, where you will purchase a home occupational license. This is a license to work from home.

You will need to fill out your business name and phone number, and give some details on the nature of your business. Most questions on the form you will fill out are designed to detect and deter people who will be a nuisance or a risk to their neighbors, and will not apply to you. This license should cost you about $100, and will be valid for one year. You will provide a photocopy of your license upon entrance to wholesale shopping establishments.

If you are not planning to be a wholesaler, you may not need to get a business license. Before deciding, see the advice from the Nolo.com article listed in the Resources section that immediately follows. The U.S. Small Business Administration also has a webpage with links to information about business licenses. It is located at **www.sba.gov/hotlist/license.html**.

Resources

- *Nolo.com Small Business Resources*
  Click on the "Business and Human Resources" tab, then select "Ownership Structures"
  www.nolo.com

- *Proprietorship, Partnership or Incorporation?* (Canadian)
  www.cbsc.org/osbw/session5/busforms.cfm

- *Quicken: Incorporate Your Business Online*
  http://quicken.incorporating.com/index.html

5.1.4 Insurance

Big businesses carry all sorts of insurance. They carry insurance on their property, its contents, the paperwork, their receivables, and even their employees' lives. You won't need to go that far. Property insurance is the first thing you need to worry about, but you may later want to consider some other forms of insurance, including disability insurance for yourself to partially replace your income if necessary.

Types of Insurance

Property Insurance

Property insurance protects the contents of your office. The cost for insuring the office equipment will probably be relatively little, and may even be handled as a rider to your homeowner's or renter's insurance. Because a lot of what you produce is "intellectual property," you might want to inquire as to how the insurance company you are considering regards paper; bills, invoices, plans you've discussed with a client and written out, etc. You may be able to add a rider to your policy to cover the cost of reconstructing these things if something happens to your office.

Errors and Omissions Insurance

This type of insurance may be useful if problems come up because you neglected to do something, thinking the client was going to do it instead. Or if you forgot to insert a liability disclaimer in a contract to buy wetsuits for a scuba expedition, and the wetsuits turned out to be defective, this sort of insurance could be useful as well.

Insurance for You

If your family depends on your income, you may want to consider life insurance or disability insurance. Other types of personal insurance include health insurance or dental insurance (if you're not covered under a spouse's plan).

Most people have some form of life insurance, but many do not have disability insurance, even if someone else employs them. It is an important form of insurance to consider, however, when you are solely responsible for your income.

You may be able to find insurance through membership in your local sales or sales executive associations. But anyone who is self-employed can find several types of relatively affordable insurance, as well as other small-business assistance, from the National Association for the Self-Employed. NASE has independent agents nationwide, so you will have access to local experts on small business insurance needs. And best of all, they are small businesspeople themselves, as they are contractors – not employees – of NASE. Visit the NASE website at **www.nase.org** to learn more.

There are other types of insurance, and many different levels of coverage are available for each type. An insurance broker (check the Yellow Pages) can advise you of your options and shop around for the best rates for you. Or you may be able to get insurance through a professional association you belong to.

In the meantime, you can find out more about business insurance from American Express at **http://home.americanexpress.com/home/ open.shtml**. Search on "Small" and "Primer" in the search box provided.

5.2 Setting Up Your Office

5.2.1 Location

Where you live will affect what type of shopping business you choose to run. For example, if you live in a town of 5,000 with only one large shopping mall, you probably can't make a living as a fashion shopper with just your local clientele – but you could look at running a personal shopping business online.

If you live in an urban or suburban area, your options are pretty much unlimited as far as setting up a personal shopping business. And after that, it's only a matter of deciding to work out of your home or rent office space.

Due to the nature of the work, most personal shoppers choose to begin at home. Many like the convenience of commuting only about 50 feet. And it does save a significant amount on start-up costs. Just renting commercial space can be costly; in addition to the first month's rent, you will probably have to pay a deposit of at least another month's rent, plus – in some areas – agent's fees and other charges. Still, the choice is up to you, depending on your business and your needs.

Working from Home

For many people, the biggest benefit of working from home is the end of the commuter lifestyle. You can take breaks when you need them, and on those breaks you can do what you need to do, from making up the bed in the guest room to playing with Fido.

Another big plus: you can deduct from your income taxes a percent of your mortgage payment and property taxes (or rent) and a share of utilities and maintenance costs. There are various methods to make those calculations, but by far the easiest – and most acceptable to the IRS – is to use an entire room, and to use it for no other purpose.

In the U.S., IRS Publication 587 has information on how to compute the calculation and file the deduction. You can download this information by visiting the IRS website and searching for the publication numbers from the search engine on the front page. (See the section on taxes later in this chapter.)

The other thing you should check before deciding on an office at home is local zoning. Most places won't have a problem with a home-based business that adds only a few cars a day to the automobile load on your street. Most will, however, prohibit you from posting a sign in your front yard, which is OK anyway, as you will not get any clients from drive-by traffic. To find out the rules in your area, look up "zoning" or "planning" in the local government section of your phone book.

In addition to any legalities, working from home requires some planning with family members. Set regular office hours that you will insist on, both for your own focus and to keep family members from intruding when you need to work. It will be tempting for the family to interrupt you. So make it clear you are at work unless it's an emergency. (The garage on fire is an emergency; Sis not being able to find her new Capri pants in the laundry is not.)

Finally, before deciding to set up a home office, make sure you have all the space you will need to run a personal shopping business. You will need:

- A large desk, preferably with enough space for a phone, your computer, vendor catalogs you use most often, and plenty of writing room

- Storage space for supplies

- Storage space for items on approval including bars to hang garments, as well as spaces for folded garments, accessories and so on

- Room to expand to accommodate a part-time assistant or perhaps a bookkeeper, when you get to that point

- A couple of guest chairs, and, if space and money permit, a conversation area with comfortable chairs and table to consult with clients

Decorate your space like an office, but don't spare the office amenities, such as coffee, tea or soft drinks, and even cookies to go with them. Strike a balance between homey and professional, but make it lean toward the professional side (i.e. no plastic toys on the floor, and set meeting times when you can have a babysitter or family member care for the children out of the business area.)

Renting Space

While a home office works well for many personal shoppers, others prefer to rent a separate space. If you find it challenging to stay motivated, or tend to get easily distracted when you're at home, an office may be just what you need to help you focus on business.
A separate space also creates a better impression if you plan to have people visit you. If you want a place to meet with clients and vendors, or work with employees, you might want to consider getting an office outside your home.

Look for a place that is convenient to get to from your home, and that gives you quick access to any services you may need. Such services might include your bank, suppliers of materials, even a good coffee shop! Pick an area that suits your needs and fits your budget. For good advice on what to consider before renting space visit Nolo.com's Small Business Resources at **www.nolo.com** and click on the "Business and Human Resources" tab; then select "Starting a Business"; then "Finding & Renting Space for Your Business".

5.2.2 Telephones

The telephone is your lifeline, your avenue to good service and a great income. In addition to your business line, you may need the following:

- A fax line (optional)

- A cell phone

- A dedicated computer line (DSL) or a cable Internet connection

Other lines you may need later include an extra line for an employee, or just an extra line for yourself if you find you must be on the phone with a vendor and a customer at the same time. You will eliminate a lot of "telephone tag" when you are trying to arrange a purchase.

Your Business Line

Your main phone number should be a business line. It will cost a little more than a residential line, but you will be listed under your business name in the white pages and under directory assistance (which makes it easy for clients to find you) and you can receive a free listing in the Yellow Pages under "Personal Shoppers." In fact, for many personal shoppers, that is the best money they spend on promotion.
Make this phone off-limits to the rest of the family. And always be sure it is answered professionally with the name of your business and "How can we help you?"

> **TIP:** Do not ask, "How can I help you?" You are running a business, and whether or not you have many employees, or none, a business is a "We." After all, you work very closely with your suppliers, and you may want to grow and include more people later.

These days, even large corporations have their phones answered by voice mail systems, so it should make little difference to your business if you either install an answering machine or subscribe to the voice-mail services offered by telephone companies.

The advantage to the answering machine is that you can monitor calls as they come in, and defer responding if what you are currently doing is more crucial than answering the phone. The advantage to the voice mail services is that they are easy to access on the road, and they offer a number of choices about how callers can leave messages. Most have message forwarding capabilities, so you can send incoming messages from your office phone to your cell phone, for example, if you decide you want to return calls while you are out.

You could also hire someone to answer the phone when you are not there. But unless you have other work for that person to accomplish, that would certainly be a lot less cost-effective than using any of the electronic helpers available. And fortunately, answering services – with real people taking messages – are just about a thing of the past. Often, the person answering the phone would not be interested in projecting the kind of image your business should project. You can perfectly control that by putting your own message on your answering machine, and you can use a few seconds of the "answer" for promotion as well.

For example, you could record a greeting that says:

> "Hello. You have reached the offices of Gotta Have It Shopping Service. No one is available to answer your call right now, but please leave your name, number and a brief message, and we will get back to you as soon as possible."

(By the way, Gotta Have It is a name used by a business that deals in collectibles. But it is the sort of catchy, descriptive name you'll need to invent for your business.) As catchy as that business name is, the message above is boring, and only marginally effective. And it does not make complete use of the technology available; in short, if you used a message like that, you would not be getting all you could for your voice mail money.

Here's another example that takes advantage of your voice mail's capability, without taking advantage of the customer:

> "Hello. Gotta Have It Shopping Service is out doing what we do best: shopping for the things that make your life a joy, a treat and a fantastic experience. But we'll be back as soon as the stores close. Please leave us your name, your phone number and the best time to reach you, and one of our experienced Gotta Have It consultants will return your call."

Or you could try this one:

> "Don't have time to get it, but you Gotta Have It? We can help. We're out shopping right now, but we'll be back when the stores close. Please leave your name, phone number and a brief message, and we'll call you back just as soon as we unpack those shopping bags with the great stuff we found for our clients. Thanks. Talk with you soon."

You can also add a line that says:

> "If you are desperate for our help right now, call our cell phone number, (555) 555-5585, or leave your number on our pager, (555) 555-8898. We will get back to you as soon as possible."

When you sign up for your voice mail or telephone service, be sure you can get an instant list of all the calls you've received since you last picked up messages. Why? Because many people don't speak clearly, or even make a mistake when they leave their voice message, and you might not be able to call them back. If you have a list of all the numbers of those who left messages, you can easily figure out which is the missing link, and call that person back. Most telephone company voice mail services offer this option, either standard or as an add-on. Some are easier than others to use, so do some investigation first.

Several phone companies, like Verizon, MCI, AT&T and Sprint, offer that service and you can review them at their respective websites. They are all national or international carriers, but you can also find good deals in regional telephone companies. For instance, Cavalier Telephone, which serves the mid-Atlantic region of the U.S., provides a complete package of services including voice mail with lots of options for as little as $29.95 per month. You can compare rates for service from many companies in your area at sites such as **www.LowerMyBills.com** and **www. 8884dialtone.com**.

Additional Phones

You can use your regular business line for faxes, or you can use your Internet line by installing software that lets you send faxes from your computer. (However, that poses a problem: What do you do when the fax is a document that isn't in your computer, and you don't want to scan into your computer?)

While it is a bit more expensive to have three lines – phone, fax and Internet – those costs are minimal in comparison to the business you might lose if you had to explain, "Well, to receive a fax, I'll have to be off the phone. So just phone to tell me when you're going to fax it."

Even if you do have a fax line, you might consider getting the software you need to fax things from your computer to a fax receiver, in case there are times you just want to send documents totally through cyberspace without using paper. For an example of a program that does this, check out WinFax Pro's website at **www.symantec.com/winfax**.

When you install your initial business phone lines, consider making the first line a rollover line that can handle two phones. That way, when there is a call on one, the next incoming call will roll over to the other phone, which your new assistant can pick up instead of having the call go to voice-mail.

You should also get a cell phone as soon as possible. As a successful personal shopper, you may spend a lot of time away from your office shopping, investigating new retailers, making arrangements with vendors, handling shipping and meeting with clients at their homes or offices.

While you may not be able to return all calls while you are on the road, you can pick and choose. The cell phone, coupled with a voice mail service and message forwarding, may help you increase your potential client contacts better than any other method.

Telephone Tips

Often, people will wait only a short time for a return call before they move on to the next company that provides what they want to buy, whether that's tires for their car or a consultant to help them update their wardrobe and purchase new things.

So make sure you honor that callback time frame everyone seems to have. For some, it's only a few minutes. Most will wait at least half a business day, however, and you should be easily able to make contact with those callers and present your business services before they have looked elsewhere.

What about call waiting? It's rude, pure and simple. Callers these days are used to leaving messages. And if someone is on the phone with you, they don't want to be asked to hold in the middle of their important conversation unless your building is on fire.

So don't get call waiting, or, if it comes in the package of services from your telephone service provider, don't use it. It's actually easier to ignore than a ringing phone. Your caller may hear a little beep as the other call tries to kick in. But if you ignore it, the caller you're speaking with will be happy, and will also think, "Wow, I'm so important, she ignored another incoming call for me!" Don't get call waiting just to impress your customers that way, though.

Likewise, do not answer your cell phone while speaking with a client or prospect at their office, or yours. (Don't answer your desk phone, either). The only exception to that would be if, during your conversation, an opportunity arose in which you could say, "Let me call the vendor, and I'll find out for you right now" and the vendor says they'll call you back in five minutes.

That makes it imperative to get a cell phone with caller ID — the only call you want to pick up in five minutes is that vendor's call, and caller ID will let you do that.

Your cell phone should have a vibrate mode, too, so that you'll know if a call did come in while you were meeting, and you can then check your messages and call back after the meeting.

5.2.3 Equipment and Supplies

What is that telephone going to sit on? Not your kitchen table. So you will have to furnish your home office and buy basic office supplies.

Basic Supplies

The supplies are easy. Office Depot and Staples are everywhere, but you can also order what you need by phone and online. And depending on the size of the items or size of the order, delivery is possible.

These stores also often run sales. Just as you might stock up on household paper goods at Sam's Club or Costco, stock up on non-perishable office supplies during specials. You'll need paper for your computer, receipt books, pens, pencils, envelopes, paper clips, sticky notes, fax toner, printer cartridges... the list goes on and on.

You might even want to go window-shopping online or in office supply catalogs as you begin setting up your business; the organizational tools they offer can be especially helpful to a new business. Daytimers, for example, come in a number of configurations. Investigating what's available may even help you set up your routines and procedures so they work best for you.

Furniture

Both retailers mentioned for basic supplies offer good prices on new office furniture. And locally, you can probably find a used or discount office furniture store. But, especially since you are in a creative business, you might want to consider the home office furniture sold by two trendy lifestyle stores, Pier One and Ikea.

Pier One has myriad stores everywhere. Ikea has fewer, but they do have a great catalog – both paper and online – and they ship. Of the two, Ikea offers more in the way of home office furniture, and it's inexpensive. You can get a computer desk, chair and lamp for under $150, and it will be stylish in a Scandinavian modern way.

Pier One doesn't have office suites, but it does have occasional pieces that can be useful in home offices, from chairs (like inexpensive director's chairs to use as guest chairs) to entertainment centers and wardrobes you might find useful for your purposes.

Computer and Software

If you don't have a computer, consider buying or leasing one for your business as soon as you can afford it. In addition to the computer, it's a good idea to get a printer, something to back up your files (such as a Zip drive or CD-RW) , and a digital camera (or a regular camera and scanner) to take and send electronic photos of your work, such as outfits you have put together, gifts purchased for individuals or businesses, etc.

Many computers already have the basic software needed to run a business. Some versions of Microsoft Office come with a suite of small business tools. You may also want to get a bookkeeping program such as Quicken or Quickbooks as well as a database program to keep track of your clients. The MS Office Small Business Suite has one, or you can buy a database program such as ACT! or Filemaker Pro. The staff at a computer store or office supplies store can give you information about specific programs and help you choose the best for you.

Photocopier

This used to be considered optional equipment for small businesses. But today, when you can get a unit that is a combination photocopier, fax machine, scanner, printer, and telephone for a few hundred dollars, you should consider getting one.

You are unlikely to need dozens of photocopies; you might need to make a copy or two of an agreement from time to time, and if you have the equipment right there, you won't have to go all the way to Kinko's to do it. And remember, time is money, especially when you have a lot to do and a lot on your mind. This business is fun, so keep excess stress as far away as you can — consider buying one of these things.

Calculator

A good desktop calculator or adding machine can make your job easier. One that makes it easy to calculate percentages would be nice, especially if you decide to charge your clients by setting fees of a percentage above the retail price of the things you purchase. A credit-card sized calculator is nice to have in your briefcase, too, for working out charges on the spot.

You might even want to consider getting a small calculator that prints. These actually do come sized to fit into a briefcase, and having a paper tape of your calculations might come in handy later when your memory temporarily checks out and you need an answer to a cost question for a client.

File Cabinet

You'll need to organize and store information you receive from vendors and keep files for each client. Lateral filing cabinets are terrific. They are easy to use and more attractive, usually, than the standard metal two- or four-drawer variety. But they are expensive, so you may want to just get serviceable cabinets to begin with and hold off on the lateral files until you make more money.

Stationery

Stationery is more than just a "supply." Your stationery will present you. Although these days we use e-mail more often, you will still need stationery for confirmation letters, inquiries from vendors, and reasons you cannot imagine right now.

You can print stationery right from your computer, and many people do. But consider this: you are in a creative business and an image business. It would be better if you had beautiful, coordinated stationery, envelopes, bills/receipts and business cards to promote your business whenever anyone receives something in the mail from you. And you might also consider adding to that a simple bi-fold brochure that describes your business and services. See section 6.2.1 for brochure ideas.

Beautiful stationery can help reassure prospective clients that you have a good eye and can help them with their image, their purchases, or their lifestyle. Consider using heavy textured papers, raised printing, and a professional design. Check around for prices at print shops or office supply stores.

If your start-up finances are limited, you might want to consider getting free business cards from VistaPrint. They offer color business cards on heavy paper stock, and a number of different designs are available. In return for the free cards (all you pay is shipping, which starts at around $7) they print their logo and "Business Cards are free at VistaPrint.com" on the back of the card near the bottom, so you still have room to write something on the back if you want to. If you don't want anything printed on the back, you can get 250 cards for only $29.95 plus shipping. Visit **www.vistaprint.com** to find out more.

This is a terrific value, and they really are fast about getting the cards to you. Be sure if you do this that the design you choose (one of many standard images provided by VistaPrint) coordinates with your stationery, or the design you have stored in your computer to print as letterhead each time you need to send a physical document rather than e-mail.

5.3 Employees and Contractors

You may be working on your own when you first start your business, but at some point you could decide to hire people to work with you. For example, you might hire an assistant, another personal shopper, or someone to help market your company. You might hire these people as employees, or you might sign them on as contractors.

As mentioned in section 3.2.1, contractors are businesses or self-employed individuals. If you provide concierge services, you will likely have a core of contractors (they may also be called subcontractors) you can call when a client needs something done such as household repairs or landscaping.

5.3.1 Differences Between Employees and Contractors

Legally, if you hire an employee, you will have to pay payroll taxes on that employee, and probably make unemployment and worker's compensation contributions to the appropriate government agency. On the other hand, you can train those employees the way you like, and you can require them to do their work at certain hours and at places you choose.

If you hire contractors, those people will have learned their job skills elsewhere. They can choose how and when to do the work. You mutually agree on what product will be delivered or what services will be performed, as well as where and when they will be performed. But you cannot require them to be at your office or anywhere else for a certain number of hours daily. It is often best to spell out what you expect and what the contractor is to do or deliver in an agreement.

Other differences between an employee and a contractor are:

- Employees work only for you. Contractors may have other clients as well as you, and can work for any and all of them.

- Employees are paid on a regular basis. Contractors are paid per project.

- Employees work for a certain number of hours. Contractors set their own hours, as long as they get the job done. That can be great for them if they are really fast, or not so great for them if they are really slow. As long as the project is finished on time to specs, it's great for you. (On the other hand, if an employee is slow, you may end up paying more salary to get the job done in overtime, or even hiring temporary help to get things finished.)

- Employees can be fired or quit. Contractors can't be fired in the usual way while they are working under contract. You may decide to have them stop working on a project, but you will be obliged to pay them according to your contractual agreement unless you are able to renegotiate the contract or successfully sue them if you are unhappy with their work. (Of course that would only be in extreme cases; it is best to avoid lawsuits altogether!)

Even though you are not writing paychecks to contractors, but rather checks for contracting fees, there are still tax considerations. To find more information about employment taxes, visit the IRS website at **www.irs.ustreas.gov**.

Before you hire anyone, check with your local department of labor to find out all the rules and regulations required as an employer. Excellent advice on hiring employees and contractors can also be found at Nolo.com's

Small Business Resources. Visit **www.nolo.com** and click on the "Business and Human Resources" tab; then select "Human Resources".

Other state and federal rules and regulations may apply to you, including: health and safety regulations, Workers' Compensation, minimum wage and unemployment insurance. You can find more information from the Small Business Administration's website at **www.sba.gov/starting/ regulations.html#othercon**.

Canadian employers must also register with the government and comply with federal and provincial laws. For information on becoming an employer in Canada, visit Canada Business Service Centres' online small business workshop at **www.cbsc.org/osbw/session5/employer.cfm**.

5.3.2 Tips for Working with Contractors

You are ultimately responsible for how well contractors do their jobs, so you will need to find people you can depend on to do the job right, by the agreed upon deadline, for the agreed upon price.

To help you choose contractors, make appointments to meet either by phone or in person. Many contractors (especially those involved in household renovations) are busy, but if you let them know when you first contact them that you have a business and would like to meet with them (or talk with them) to find out about their services and fees with the possibility of hiring them for future projects, they are more likely to take the time to discuss what they can offer.

Ask what services they provide, their rates, and their availability. For example, you will need to know if they are available on short notice, if they can only fit you in on week-ends, and what will happen to your project if another project they are working on ends up taking more time than they expected. You need to know that you can depend on the contractor, and that they will be willing to work overtime if necessary to keep their agreements with you. (Unfortunately, some busy contractors consider deadlines to be "suggestions" rather than requirements.)

As the personal shopper or concierge it will be your job to supervise them and ensure they get the job done. Remember your name (not the contractor's) is on the line if you bring in a contractor to do any work and they don't come through in a timely or professional manner or within cost. So look for someone reliable, and have at least one back-up for each job.

Wherever possible, get agreements (e.g. for costs, delivery dates, services to be provided) in writing. Also check if the contractor holds liability insurance, which covers both them and you in the event that the client's property is damaged, or that the work is not satisfactory for some reason.

Before working with a contractor, check their references. It is also advisable to contact the Better Business Bureau to find out if any complaints have been lodged against them or their company. To locate a BBB anywhere in the U.S. or Canada visit their website at **www.bbb.org**.

5.4 Financial Matters

5.4.1 Start-Up Funding

If you begin your business as a personal shopper in your own home, your start-up costs can be almost nothing. Because you are spending your clients' money, you can get a deposit from them to cover purchases, or it may be possible for the vendor to bill them directly.

You may also be able to get local vendors to send you items "on approval" for your clients to look at before buying. (See section 3.2 for more information about working with vendors.) However, even if you don't have upfront costs for merchandise, you may have other costs, such as promotional costs and office expenses. If so, you will need some working capital until the fees from your clients begin rolling in.

Many entrepreneurs are optimistic about how much money they will earn from their business, and that's a good thing. Set your goals high. But don't be as optimistic about how quickly you will earn it. While you may be tremendously successful right from the start and exceed your own expectations, it is wise to be prepared for the possibility that it may take longer than expected until your business earns enough to support you. A standard rule of thumb is to have six months' living expenses set aside beyond your start-up costs. Or you might consider remaining at your current job and working part-time on your personal shopper business until it is established.

Depending on the start-up costs you calculate in your business plan, you may find you have all the money you need to get started in your savings account (or available to spend on your credit cards). If your own resources won't cover all the things you would like to do with your business, you will need to look for financing.

One place to look for financing is from family members. They may be willing to invest in your company or give you a loan to help you get started. To avoid any misunderstandings, it's wise to get any agreements in writing even with family members.

If you decide to approach a bank for a business loan, be prepared. They will want to see a loan proposal that includes these five things:

- How much money you want

- How long do you want the money (i.e. the term of the loan before repayment)

- What you are going to do with the money

- How you will repay the loan

- Collateral (assets you could sell to repay the bank if you don't have enough money to make the payments)

When you prepare this document, ask for a little more money than you need. No matter how good their business plan is, most people underestimate the amount of money they need. It is very difficult to go back to the bank and get more money when you've just gotten some. So get all you need at once, even if it seems like a little more than you need.

You can find some additional advice about financing from the Small Business Administration at **www.sba.gov/financing/index.html.** Information is also available from Nolo.com's Small Business Legal Encyclopedia at **www.nolo.com/encyclopedia/sb_ency.html** (click on "Business Financing").

5.4.2 Keeping Track of Your Finances

If you are one of those people who seldom enters checks you've written into your check register, now is the time to get with it, at least as far as your business goes. Here are some tactics to use to keep track of your business income and outgo, and keep it separate from your own money.

Open a business account at a bank, trust company or credit union, even if you are using only your own name to do business. And use this only for paying the bills of the company and your own salary, which you then deposit in your personal account.

Get a style of business check that makes it impossible for you not to record checks you've written. And avoid using electronic payments. You want to create a paper trail for your business account so you are able to:

- Prove your deductions at tax time

- Create balance sheets that your vendors or other financial institutions may request from time to time

- See at a glance where your money has gone

Also, keep track of your accounts receivable, accounts payable, and so on in a ledger book, which you can get at any office supply store. Or else use an electronic bookkeeping package. The most popular bookkeeping software for small business is Quicken. For under a hundred dollars, Quicken's Premier Home and Business program will help you prepare invoices, manage your accounts, and generate reports from your records. Find out more about Quicken software at **www.quicken.com/ quickensw**.

Finally, keep two additional ledgers – small enough to carry in your purse or briefcase – so you can log: (1) mileage or other travel expenses, and (2) everything you spend during the day (remember to keep personal and business expenses separate).

Also carry an envelope so you can keep receipts for everything you buy for the business and everything you must pre-purchase or put a deposit on for a client. Be sure to re-file these at night in the appropriate files in your file cabinet. The business receipts should be stapled to the order form for each purchase/service for a client. No matter how you design a system, make sure it works for you and that you can find receipts for anything at any time without calling in a psychic to help you figure out where you put it.

Personal/Business Lines of Credit

When you're just starting out, you will probably not get a line of credit or a credit card for your business without being backed up by your personal credit history. If you have problems in that area, you may need a partner whose credit is sterling if you decide a business line of credit is necessary.

But if it's just a matter of needing to pay by credit card, an ATM card can act as a credit card, as long as it has a MasterCard, Visa or Discover logo on it. And most banks issue them with business bank accounts.

Of course, you'll have to use your cash flow or your initial financing to cover purchases because it is not really a credit card, although it acts like one when you are making a purchase. Just think of your balance on any given day as your credit line, and you can "charge" up to that amount. While it doesn't give you additional financing as a true credit card would, it does give you some benefits of a credit card in terms of product liability, and it lets you purchase things online.

5.4.3 Taxes

Even before you begin making a profit, you've got to think about taxes. As a business owner, you will have to think about your own income tax, payroll taxes on any employees you hire, and, if you are incorporated, a corporation tax.

Tax Returns

If your business is a sole proprietorship or partnership in the United States, you will file a Schedule C with your personal tax returns. You'll also have to file a form to determine the amount you owe on your social security. (Canadians will do the same with CPP.)

That amount may surprise you. If you have been employed, you are used to paying FICA, or Social Security taxes. If you are self-employed, the amount of FICA you'll pay on the same amount of income doubles. Why? Because when you were employed, the employer paid half, so only half was deducted from your paycheck. It's a little daunting at first. But look at it this way: If you know about that up front, you can price your services accordingly.

The other thing you will want to do regarding taxes, right at the start, is apply for an Employee Identification Number (EIN). You will need this for reporting payroll taxes if you have employees. If you set up wholesale accounts, you will also need it in order to be charged for the wholesale rate, rather than the retail rate, for any items you buy to sell to your customers.

Taxes on Product Sales

While many personal shoppers simply buy items for their clients using the client's credit or by receiving cash up front, a few buy the items wholesale and then resell them at retail to their customers.

In most jurisdictions, if you buy items or services at wholesale prices and then resell them to your clients for a higher price, you will need to collect sales tax and turn it over to the appropriate city, county, state, and/or country. In order to collect sales tax, you must have a resale number. Also known as a tax number, a resale permit, or a sales tax permit, you are required to show this number on a certificate when you want to shop wholesale.

You will not pay sales tax at the point of purchase, but will file your purchases with the state or county and mail them a check.

This application should also be available at the Occupational License Office, but you will register it with either the county or the state, depending on where you live. Again, you will have to fill out a short form with information about the nature of your business. There is usually no charge to register, and the certificate will be mailed out to you within a few weeks.

Either quarterly or monthly, you will fill out a form that lists the total retail dollar amount (not wholesale amount) of the merchandise you purchased during the relevant period of time, calculate the tax owed, and mail in a check. File these forms on time, or you risk being assessed some hefty fines and interest on the amount owing.

It is very important to note that the tax is on the resale value, not the wholesale price. When you shop for wholesale items, you will want to make a habit of noting the retail price. If there is no retail price listed where you purchase the item, you can assume to double the wholesale price to get the retail.

In turn, you will also collect the sales tax from your clients, so you won't be out the money unless you sell to your clients at a marked down price. In some states and provinces you will also be eligible for a vendor's compensation (commission), which means that you can keep a very small percentage of the tax you collect as payment for being a "government agent."

When you purchase items wholesale, you may also be asked to fill out a blanket certificate of resale by the seller. This simply means that you understand the situation and agree to pay the sales tax on the items you purchase.

In Canada, the process is quite similar. You will want to contact your provincial Department of Finance to apply for a vendor's license or permit for the purpose of collecting provincial sales tax (applicable in most provinces). Also, businesses with revenue exceeding $30,000 must register with the Canada Revenue Agency for a business number in order to collect the Goods and Services Tax. Check out the CRA's website at **www.cra-arc.gc.ca** to find out more.

If you are able to do business entirely by using your clients' credit accounts, or if they reimburse you for anything you buy for them, you may not need a sales tax license. However, your services may be taxable, and you'll have to collect taxes on those fees and turn them over to the appropriate agency. To find out which taxes apply in your jurisdiction, check the resources below and consult with an accountant:

- *Nolo.com Small Business Resources*
  Click on the "Business and Human Resources" tab; then select "Making a Profit; then "Saving Business Taxes"
  www.nolo.com

- *Canada Revenue Agency*
  www.cra-arc.gc.ca/tax/business/smallbusiness

Some business owners erroneously think that they can avoid paying sales tax on office supplies and other items they use within their businesses. That is not so; a business pays sales tax on anything it uses except those things they directly resell. If you were reselling paper – for instance, if a client asked you to get him 5,000 reams of chartreuse printer paper – then you would buy it at wholesale without paying sales tax and you would collect that tax from your client, who is buying it from you at retail. If you bought one ream of chartreuse paper and intended to use it for your own solicitation letters – even though you were using it to run your business – you would still pay sales tax for it.

You can take a look at the rules at your own state's website, which you can find at **www.taxsites.com/state.html**.

5.4.4 Setting Your Fees

Long before your first phone call from a prospective client, you need to decide how much you will charge for your time and expertise. The most common ways for personal shoppers to charge for their services are one or more of the following:

- A percentage

- An hourly fee

- A daily or half-day fee

Percentage of Price

This method involves charging clients a percentage of the price of the merchandise you buy for them (before taxes). Many personal shoppers use this method, alone or in combination with an hourly fee.

Generally, the fee will vary depending on the total amount spent. While the percentage amount usually ranges from 10% to 25% of the retail price, we found personal shoppers who charge as little as 5% for a large purchase, and as much as 30% for a small purchase.

Below are some sample fees charged by several personal shoppers. The first buys relatively expensive items, while the other two buy more low cost items.

Personal Shopper No. 1

- 10 percent for purchases up to $5,000

- 7 percent for purchases of $5,000-$10,000

- 5 percent for purchases over $10,000

Personal Shopper No. 2

- $25 plus 10 percent on purchases up to $200

- 25 percent on purchases from $200 to $500

- 20 percent on purchases of $500 or more

Personal Shopper No. 3

- 30 percent on purchases up to $200

- 25 percent on purchases over $200

NOTE: This personal shopper sells a particular manufacturer's products (in addition to providing other personal shopping services) and there is no personal shopping fee if the items are from that company's product line. On those purchases, the personal shopper earns the difference between the wholesale and the retail price as her fee.

Before deciding to charge a fee based on a percentage of the merchandise price, do some calculations to ensure that it makes sense for you financially. While it can certainly be profitable if you are dealing only with wealthy clients who regularly purchase thousands of dollars worth of merchandise, you will need to decide if it is worthwhile to work this way if you take clients who are spending a lot less.

For example, if you charge 25%, and it takes two hours of your time (including research, driving to a store, meeting with the client, etc.) to purchase a $200 item, you would be earning $50 or only $25 per hour. However, charging this way may be worthwhile if you do a lot of your shopping online, by catalog or telephone. By locating your merchandise before you actually go (or by simply arranging for delivery), you can make this method more profitable.

If you charge a percentage, it is wise to have a minimum fee (such as $25, $50 or more) in case your client changes their mind and decides not to purchase anything. Another option, to ensure you are well compensated for your time, is to charge an hourly fee.

Hourly Fees

An hourly fee is another common way for personal shoppers to charge for their services. A few who are in great demand to work with wealthy clients command fees of hundreds of dollars per hour. One example is New-York based Visual Therapy (**www.visual-therapy.com**), an image consulting company that has been featured on the Oprah TV show, and in numerous fashion magazines. As of April, 2005, their rate for personal shopping services was $450 per hour or 20% of the retail price, whichever amount is more.

While you may be able to charge hundreds of dollars per hour if you have wealthy clients and extensive experience, most personal shoppers charge fees ranging from $25 to $100 per hour. A 2001 article in *Best of New York* magazine on personal shoppers gave the example of another personal shopping company, Cross It Off Your List:

> "For $75 per hour (they) will take care of your more utilitarian shopping, like buying all the necessities for a new apartment, setting up your beach house for the summer, and buying gifts for everyone on your Christmas list."

You do not have to start at $25 per hour. In fact, you may want to charge a higher fee when you start because it may actually make certain clients more likely to work with you. Many professionals believe "you get what you pay for" so they may assume a personal shopper who charges $50 per hour will provide better services than one who charges $25 per hour.

On the other hand, if you are providing grocery shopping services for senior citizens, they will very likely not want to pay anywhere near the amount paid by wealthy women who hire you to buy designer clothing, or corporations that hire you to purchase gifts for their clients. So you will need to consider your target markets when deciding what fees to charge. (See the next chapter for information on target markets.) With clients such as senior citizens it is probably better to stick with a percentage fee. And remember that you can change your fees in the future if you change your clientele or as you get more experience.

If you charge by the hour, you could also charge for your travel time and any time you spend waiting for deliveries. However, some professionals do not charge for local travel, or charge a lower fee for travel time (e.g. if their hourly fee is $50 per hour they might charge $25 per hour for travel).

Daily Rates

If you are working with wealthy individuals or corporate clients who will be hiring you for lengthier projects, you may want to consider a daily fee (also known as a per diem). By offering a daily rate that works out to a little less than your hourly fee, you may encourage clients to hire you for longer periods of time. For example, your fee structure might look like this:

Length of Consultation	Fee
Full day (up to 6 hours)	$500
Half day (up to 3 hours)	$250
Hourly	$100

An article titled "Personal shoppers aren't just for the rich anymore," the Middletown, NewYork *Times Herald-Record* reported the fees of personal shopping business I've Been Dressed as follows:

"Fees range from $500 for a five-hour day spent with a personal shopper (that includes a light lunch and transportation), $300 for a half day, and $100 per hour of shopping time when the client is off-site" (i.e. when the personal shopper shops without the client).

However, that's not the highest daily rate we found. Wealthy clients pay Susan Tabak $1,500 per day for shopping trips to Paris (see section

6.1). This fee includes Susan as your personal shopper and transportation around the city. Lunch on your first day and dinner on your last is also included.

Whatever fees you decide to charge, to ensure you get paid, consider having your clients sign an agreement (see section 5.5 for sample agreements). In the next section you will see several ways to arrange for payment, both for merchandise and your services.

5.4.5 Arranging Payment

Paying for the Client's Purchases

There are several options for paying for merchandise purchased for a client:

When You Shop with the Client

When you and the client go shopping together, you should have the client pay for all their purchases. How clients pay is up to them. They may pay by cash, credit card, or any other method the merchant accepts.

When You Shop for an Individual

It is a good idea to ask for the client's credit card number so you can charge any purchases you make for the client, either online or over the telephone. If the client is not willing to give you their credit card number, or if you will be making purchases in person, you will need to arrange another method of payment. Your options include:

- Have clients pay you in advance if you will be picking up and delivering items to them

- Have clients pay upon delivery

- Have clients go in person to the store to review items you have put on hold for them, and pay for any they wish to purchase

A few personal shoppers prefer to pay for items up front, then charge the client for the purchases and their fees in a single bill. However, if you pay up front for any client purchases make sure you do not risk your own funds. Ensure that all purchases are fully returnable with no restocking fees. And do not do any purchasing this way without a written agreement. (See section 5.5 for information about contracts.)

When You Shop for a Corporate Client

As mentioned in section 3.2, most vendors will expect to be paid at least 50% for items before they ship them. However, if you are purchasing for a major corporation that has good credit, the vendor may ship the merchandise to your client without pre-payment, and invoice the client directly.

If you do not arrange for the vendor to invoice the client, you will need to either: (1) get a company check or credit card number from your client to pay the vendor, or (2) cover the cost yourself and invoice the client later for both your fee and the cost of the merchandise.

In most cases, you should not need to pay for the merchandise yourself. However, if you have an ongoing relationship with a client, or the item is not expensive, you might decide to take the risk. Just as you would with an individual client, make sure you have a written agreement with the client. Also follow the advice in the section below on accepting checks.

Corporate clients are usually invoiced at the end of a project, or they can be invoiced monthly if a project is ongoing. A challenge with invoicing is that corporations normally expect at least 30 days to pay, and some wait 60 or 90 days before putting a check in the mail. So you may want to ask for a deposit (such as 50%) up front.

Your invoice should be on your letterhead and include the following items:

- The client name and contact information

- A purchase order number (if the client gave you one)

- A list of services you provided with the date and cost

- Any expenses and taxes payable

- The total amount due

- Terms of payment (e.g. "Payable within 30 days")

Sample Invoice

(On Your Letterhead)

INVOICE

DATE: November 5, 2006

TO: Carla Client
Marketing Department
XYZ Corporation
123 Main Street
Sunnyday, CA 90211

RE: Holiday Gift Shopping for XYZ's Clients

50 gold-plated widgets (@ $25 each)	$1,250.00
50 engravings (@ $15 each)	$750.00
Gift shopping services: client meetings, gift recommendations, order processing, coordinating production and delivery (2 days @ $500 per day)	$1,000.00
10% Tax *(use your own tax rate here)*	300.00
Subtotal	$3,000.00
Less Deposit	($1,500.00)
Total – Please pay this amount	**$1,800.00**

TERMS: Payable within 30 days.

Thank you for your business.

Getting Paid

You have a variety of options for getting paid by your client.

Accepting Debit Cards

With a debit purchase, the funds come directly out of the client's account at the bank and are deposited directly into your business bank account. There is no credit involved for customer or merchant. That being so, you probably won't have to do much more than ask your business banker for an application in order to accept debit card purchases.

There may be a short delay or small charge to you, initially or ongoing, depending on the bank. You will have to get the equipment to process the payments and print receipts. (Federal law mandates receipts be provided to customers for debit card purchases.) The equipment costs between $200 and $500, or you may be able to lease it on a monthly basis.

Accepting Credit Cards

American Express and Discover cards set up merchant accounts nationally and internationally. MasterCard and Visa are local; to become a merchant accepting those, you will have to get accepted by a local financial institution (an "acquiring bank").

Because yours is a new business, you may have to shop around to find one that gives you good rates (you will be charged between 1.5 and 3 percent per transaction for the service, and often an initial setup fee and perhaps ongoing fees for phone calls, postage, statements and so on).

You might also have to provide a good personal financial record to set up an advantageous rate, at least until you've become established in your business and have a good track record for them to look at. Remember, the bank is granting you credit in this instance, "banking" on the fact that your clients will not want refunds or that you won't try to keep the money if they do.

These days, although the acquiring bank will be a local bank somewhere, it need not be in your hometown. Numerous services are available online to help you set up a merchant account. Companies like Merchant Bank Network (**http://mastercard-visa.com/creditcardprocess.htm**) and Electronic Transfer, Inc. (**www.electronic transfer.com**) handle setup of MasterCard and Visa accounts, as well as American Express and Discover. Applications are handled online or by fax and phone.

If a business needs to choose between accepting Discover or American Express, many choose American Express. The American Express card is more widely accepted by merchants, especially internationally, which means more customers who travel widely carry that card. It also has a reputation as the card of people who have good incomes. Originally, American Express required the entire balance to be paid off each month, so that Amex's "exposure" was only 30 days or so. If the cardholder didn't pay in a timely fashion, use of the card was suspended until that was corrected. Now, American Express also offers true charge cards as well.

Accepting Payment Online

If you have a website or do online shopping for clients, another possibility is to accept payments online through services such as PayPal (**www. paypal.com**). Typically, these services charge a greater "discount rate," which is what the 1.5 to 3 percent the banks and credit card companies hold from your payments is called. And the purchase must be made online. Still, there may be instances when you are doing business online with some of your clients, and it may be useful then.

Also, it provides a safe route for conveying financial information over the Internet. If your website has a shopping cart not serviced by PayPal or another service with visible security in place, customers might not think it is safe enough.

Accepting Checks

Taking checks is a fairly safe way to accept payment. First of all, you will probably work with local individuals and businesses, or the local facilities of even multinational corporations. There is some safety in that, if they value their reputation.

But sometimes an individual has financial woes – a layoff, downsizing, life trauma – that could suddenly affect you. Due to a business down-turn, a corporation may suddenly become unreliable about their checks. So do a little background work on the reputation of companies paying you for services. Check the back issues of the *Wall Street Journal* and local business pages, as well as Hoover's Online. The *Wall Street*

Journal's website (**http://online.wsj.com/public/us**) offers searches by business name, but you will only get whatever information the newspaper has recently published about the company. Archival searches require a fee-based subscription. In-depth information from Hoover's (**www.hoovers.com**) requires paid membership, but basic information – which may be all you need to begin – is free.

When you accept checks, especially ones to cover a season's wardrobe purchases or big-ticket items or major corporate purchases, you may want to establish a credit limit for each client. The limit should partially reflect your trust in them, but it should also be one which, if they did fail to pay, would mean you still had enough cash flow from your other clients to cover your expenses.

You can accept checks from individual clients with greater assurance by using a check payment service such as TeleCheck. TeleCheck compares checks you receive with a database of over 51 million bad check records, allowing you to decide whether to accept a check from a particular client. The company also provides electronic payment services, from telephone debit card processing to electronic checks. You can find out more about TeleCheck at **www.telecheck.com**.

5.5 Client Contracts

Your contract or agreement (which may be in the form of an "engagement letter") should spell out what services you will provide for the client, when you will provide them (the dates between which or by which your services are to be completed), as well as when and how you are to be paid. The contract should also include your company name and address, as well as the contact name, company name (if applicable) and address of your client.

On the pages that follow you will find two sample contracts. The first is a standard "engagement letter" you might use with an individual client. You could ask your clients to sign it at your initial meeting, or have them return it to you later. The second is a lengthier contract which you could adapt for use with a corporate client. It covers a number of additional areas, such as a product/service liability disclaimer so that you cannot be held responsible for defects in items you buy or services you subcontract for your clients. You can adapt these contracts to fit your needs. Before using them, remember to have them reviewed by your attorney.

Standard Engagement Letter

[Insert name of Client]
[Insert address of Client]

[Date]

Dear [Name of client],

As promised, I have set out below a description of the services that [your name/company] will provide to you.

I will provide the following services:
[Insert description of the services: this may include a wardrobe consultation, proposal of additions to wardrobe, plan for purchasing and so on.]

Please note that I will not be providing these services:
[Insert description of the services that will not be provided; these may include alterations, laundering, etc.]

My fee for the services performed will be as follows:
[Insert rates. If you will be passing on such costs as shipping and returns directly, state that here.]

If required, a note can be sent to you every [week/month/quarter], detailing the actual time spent providing the services to you.

If you agree that the foregoing fairly sets out your understanding of our mutual responsibilities, please sign a copy of this letter in the space indicated below, and return it to me at [insert address, fax number or e-mail address].

Yours sincerely,
[Name]

Agreed and Accepted:

_____
[Insert name of client]

_____
Date

Standard Services Agreement

THIS AGREEMENT is made this [date] day of [month], 20__.

BETWEEN
[insert name of your client] (the "Client"), and [insert your name or your company's name] (the "Personal Shopper"), collectively referred to as the "Parties."

1.1 Services

The Personal Shopper shall provide the following services ("Services") to the Client in accordance with the terms and conditions of this Agreement: [Insert a description of the services here].

1.2 Delivery of the Services

• Start date: The Personal Shopper shall commence the provision of the Services on [insert date here].

• Completion date: The Personal Shopper shall [complete/cease to provide] the Services [by/on] [insert date here] ("Completion Date").

• Key dates: The Personal Shopper agrees to provide the following parts of the Services at the specific dates set out below: [insert dates here, such as the date for the wardrobe consultation, the fittings, replacement of items that do not fit, etc.].

1.3 Site

The Personal Shopper shall provide the Services at the following site(s): [insert details here if applicable, such as client's home, your office, etc.]

1.4 Fees

As consideration for the provision of the Services by the Personal Shopper, the fees for the provision of the Services are [insert fees here] ("Fees").

The Client [shall/shall not] pay for the Personal Shopper's out-of-pocket expenses comprising [insert here, if agreed].

1.5 Payment

The Client agrees to pay the Fees to the Personal Shopper on the following dates: [also specify whether the price will be paid in one payment, in installments or upon completion of specific milestones].

The Personal Shopper shall invoice the Client for the Services that it has provided to the Client [monthly/weekly/after the Completion Date]. The Client shall pay such invoices [upon receipt /within 30 days of receipt] from the Personal Shopper.

Any charges payable under this Agreement are exclusive of any applicable taxes, duties, or other fees charged by a government body and such shall be payable by the Client to the Personal Shopper in addition to all other charges payable hereunder.

1.6 Warranty

The Personal Shopper represents and warrants that [she/he] will perform the Services with reasonable skill and care.

1.7 Limitation of Liability

Subject to the Client's obligation to pay the Fees to the Personal Shopper, either party's liability arising directly out of its obligations under this Agreement and every applicable part of it shall be limited in aggregate to the Fees. The Personal Shopper assumes no liability due to the quality of items or services purchased for the Client.

1.8 Term and Termination

This Agreement shall be effective on the date hereof and shall continue until the completion date stated in section 1.2 unless terminated sooner. If the Client terminates this agreement for any reason before the scheduled completion date, the Client will reimburse the Personal Shopper for all outstanding fees and out-of-pocket expenses.

1.9 Relationship of the Parties

The Parties acknowledge and agree that the Services performed by the Personal Shopper, its employees, sub-contractors, or agents shall be as an independent contractor and that nothing in this Agreement shall be deemed to constitute a partnership, joint venture, or otherwise between the parties.

1.10 Confidentiality

Neither Party will disclose any information of the other which comes into their possession under or in relation to this Agreement and which is of a confidential nature.

1.11 Miscellaneous

The failure of either party to enforce its rights under this Agreement at any time for any period shall not be construed as a waiver of such rights.

If any part, term or provision of this Agreement is held to be illegal or unenforceable neither the validity or enforceability of the remainder of this Agreement shall be affected.

This Agreement constitutes the entire understanding between the Parties and supersedes all prior representations, negotiations or understandings.

Neither Party shall be liable for failure to perform any obligation under this Agreement if the failure is caused by any circumstances beyond its reasonable control, including but not limited to acts of God, war, or industrial dispute.

This Agreement shall be governed by the laws of the jurisdiction in which the Personal Shopper is located.

Agreed by the Parties hereto:

SIGNED by _____

on behalf of _____
                        [the Client]
SIGNED by _____

on behalf of _____
                        [the Personal Shopper]

6. Getting Clients

Joan Miller of Owings Mills, Maryland, has all the business she wants for her personal shopping/image/wardrobe service, and she does no marketing at all. Miller sold women's apparel at Saks for 15 years. When that store closed, most of her clients came with her. She hadn't been a personal shopper at Saks, but her clientele trusted her taste and judgment, so when she was without a job, she was not without people calling to ask her how she could help them.

She does have a Yellow Pages ad, but that's it. She does not do public speaking, and she doesn't write books. In fact, she just invites her clients to "trunk shows" she hosts at her home every season (shows where customers can see a designer's line), handles their wardrobe problems as they call for consultation, and plays bridge. It's perfect, she says, in every way.

If you haven't enjoyed the sort of career Miller has, you'll have to do some marketing. Below are some of the best ways to market a personal shopping business. Once you've gotten your first bunch of clients with these methods, you may not have to do much more to keep yourself as busy as you want to be, or busier!

6.1 Choose Your Target Markets

Before you start trying to sell your services to prospective clients, you should decide which types of clients you want to shop for. These are your "target" markets.

It can be tempting for a new personal shopper to say something like "I want to work for anyone who'll pay me!" Avoid the temptation. It is costly and time-consuming to try to market your business to "everyone" and the truth is that some people will be more interested than others in the services you have to offer. In fact, people are more likely to hire you if they see you as an "expert" who specializes in what they need.

When you are just starting out, of course you might take whatever business comes your way. However, you can focus your marketing efforts on the target markets you most want to work with. Once you start getting more business, you may be able to give up work you find less rewarding, and spend your time on clients and projects you find most rewarding.

Here are some types of markets you might consider targeting:

Individuals

In addition to the special types of shopping discussed in section 2.2, you can further refine your services by offering them to a specific group of people. The categories you target may be broad (e.g. women) or narrow (e.g. working women in their 30s). Here are a few examples:

- Tourists

- New home buyers

- The wealthy

- Senior citizens

- Working professionals

- Working mothers

- Large families

- Disabled people

- Husbands (e.g. for Valentine's or anniversaries)

- People who are redecorating

- Young entrepreneurs

Corporate Clients

Following are some examples of corporate clients you can work for, and types of services you might provide:

- Gift-buying for corporations

- Providing concierge services for corporations, small hotels, apartment complexes, or gated communities

- Purchasing products and services for employee recognition programs

- Putting together gift bags for event planners to use at events such as awards shows, conferences, conventions, and festivals

6.2 Promotional Tools

The promotional tools that can help market your business begin with your business card, but may also include a brochure, portfolio, and website.

6.2.1 Brochures

You will have many opportunities to give out your business card. In fact, you should get in the habit of giving it to almost everyone you meet. But there are also times to give out brochures. For example, when you give a presentation at a networking meeting (see section 6.3.1) or when people seem particularly interested in your services.

You should also provide some to the retailers with whom you do a lot of business. Your major vendors should have some, in case someone asks them to recommend a personal shopper, and also just so they get to know more quickly the sorts of things they can help you with.

A Niche for Those Who Love Travel and Fashion

A unique career path is the one chosen by Susan Tabak, the "Paris Personal Shopper." Tabak fell in love with France as a young girl, took a year of her college education there, and, for the past 20 years, has gone back as often as she possibly could to delve into the shopping and fashion delights of the City of Light. Now she offers shopping trips to Paris beginning at $1,500 a day. This fee includes Susan as your personal shopper. You can find out more about Susan at **www.parispersonalshopper.com**.

If you have a love and knowledge of any other world-class city known for fashion, you might do something similar. You could do it as your main business, or offer it as a part of your business – the most exciting part – if you generate a sufficient number of clients who love to travel and can afford designer clothes. What are some of the other places you could take shoppers and earn both fees and big-time excitement? Well, there's:

- **London**: The days of excitement over wedding gowns for royal princesses are over, but London fashion is still a vibrant fashion center.

- **New York City**: For those who want to visit a fashion capital without going overseas, New York has lots of world-class stores.

- **Milan**: Very chic, new designers, very big for cosmetics.

Other cities are also becoming world-class fashion destinations, and if you know them, you could make a business of leading shoppers to their best stores. Some up-and-coming fashion cities are Toronto, Tokyo, Madrid, Amsterdam and Dublin.

There are many other "niches" or target markets. Your target market may change over time as you develop your business and find you most enjoy working with particular types of clients. Often, too, the people who use your services and expertise for their business needs will call upon you for personal gifts as well (and vice versa).

Your brochure will contain your company name and contact information, including your web address. It can also include some of the information you have on your website, such as:

- Photographs of outfits, rooms, gift packages, meals or anything else you have created as part of your buying and consulting services.

- A list of the benefits of hiring a personal shopper, such as making wise choices, saving money, looking great, saving time, etc.

- A list of the services you perform, such as wardrobe analysis, gift shopping, grocery shopping, and so on.

- Your business photograph. (Do not use a "glamour shot". Have a photo taken with your hair, makeup if applicable, and clothes selected to emphasis your business side, but with flair.)

- Some comments from satisfied customers or, if those are not available yet, some comments from respected people on your integrity, abilities and so on.

Your brochure can be a bi-fold or tri-fold, in black and white or color. If you can afford it, have a commercial printer print them. They often offer design services, too, either for free or for a modest cost. Or you can design your brochure yourself on your computer using brochure paper from a stationery store. In fact, you can simply print and fold a few at a time, at first. They will not look as polished as commercially printed brochures, but they can help you get your business off the ground.

> **TIP:** Be sure you spell-check and grammar-check everything. Personal shopping clients tend to be intelligent and selective people, and they may move on to another personal shopper because of this sort of error. Check your phone number, address and e-mail address extra well. Those must be right or you'll never even know how much business you lost from frustrating your would-be clients.

When you decide you do need professionally printed brochures, check the Yellow Pages under "Printers" or use quick-printer services such as Kinko's or Minuteman Press or even the printing services of your local office supply store.

6.2.2 Presentation Portfolio

Another promotional tool that will help you secure clients is a presentation portfolio. In this, you can keep glossy photos of some of your best purchases, along with documentation of where they were purchased, and why they were selected.

It is important to have a show-and-tell presentation for meetings, especially if you deal with more than one decision-maker. That way, one person can look through your portfolio while you discuss terms with the other.

If you are focusing on fashion shopping, before-and-after photos of your clients and their outfits are especially appealing. Show how you selected clothing that looked fabulous, emphasized the client's best features, etc. You can do the same selecting furniture or home furnishings... just get the client's permission to photograph the existing sofa or bedroom suite, and then take an impressive photo of the purchases you selected all set up.

If you don't yet have any work experience, you can create a portfolio of items you theoretically would select for different types of clients in a variety of styles, to showcase your versatility. Neatly clip unique items from catalogs or magazines, and paste them in an attractive layout on a presentation board or binder. You can update this frequently as styles change, or once you get work experience.

Your portfolio should also contain your brochure, as well as any other items that would show off your expertise. For example, if the local newspaper profiles your new business (many will do this if asked), clip the article and include it. If not, write an announcement you would have liked them to print, and include that, mocked up in a newspaper style.

If anyone you have shopped for, even family and friends, has sent you a letter thanking you for your excellent job purchasing items for them, include that. Preferably they will have a different name than yours, and will not mention that you worked for free. Every time you have a satisfied client, you can add to your testimonial collection.

You can buy a portfolio case to display these items at an art supply or office supply store (check the Yellow Pages). Portfolio cases come in a variety of sizes (e.g. 11" x 14", 14" x 17", 17" x 22") and cost from about $15 to over $150, depending on the size and material. However, customers are interested in what is inside the case, so you don't need to spend a lot of money on the case itself.

Model Release Form

Whenever you publish photos of your real clients – in print or on your website – be sure you have them sign a model release form, which gives you permission to use the images in any of your promotional materials without remuneration.

Most people are happy to have their image used in such a positive way, but there may be exceptions. Asking gives them the opportunity to say they'd rather not participate, which is fine. People are entitled to their privacy, and you'll find lots of others who'd like to help.

Sample Model Release Form

I hereby give (insert your name) permission to use my photograph taken of me on (insert date) at (insert location) for promotional, on-line or commercial purposes. I am of legal age.

_____
(Print Name)

_____
(Signature)

_____
(Date)

6.2.3 Your Website

A website gives prospective clients the opportunity to preview your services 24 hours a day.

If you've never developed a website before – and relatively few people have – you won't have to spend a lot to do the job well. You may already have Microsoft Front Page or Netscape Composer (which comes free with the Netscape browser) installed on your computer. Both of those are relatively simple to use to create an attractive website.

But then you have to upload (send) the files to a server. The good news is that you don't have to be a computer genius to do this. You can use one of the many full-service companies that register your domain name (e.g. sharonshopper.com), host your website for a small monthly fee and submit it to search engines so clients can find you. One of these companies is Network Solutions at **www.netsol.com**.

You can find out about other, similar companies by visiting *Webhost Magazine*'s website. *Webhost Magazine* offers free, unbiased consumer reports on domain name registrars and web hosting companies. It also has a tutorial guide you can use to educate yourself about everything you need to know when it comes to the Internet and setting up a website. Check it out at **www.webhostmagazine.com/bg**.

> **TIP:** Avoid using free web hosting sites. They will bombard visitors to your site with pop-up ads that can turn off prospective clients.

Here are a few tips for creating your website. To get additional ideas for your website, visit those of other personal shoppers by doing an Internet search for Personal Shoppers.

- Do include all the information your brochure contains.

- Do make it visually attractive. Clients will judge your taste and style by what they see on your website. If necessary, consider hiring a professional web designer.

- Consider adding some elements that aren't in your brochure (e.g. photos from your portfolio, a fashion quiz, a top 10 list, the latest trends, shopping lists, etc.)

- Be sure you ask for the order. (For instance, say "Personal shopping works best in person. E-mail or phone me to set up a coffee meeting at The Bean Machine – my treat! – and we'll start you on the path to your perfect image without delay!")

- Be sure it contains your contact information: e-mail address, phone and fax numbers, and your "snailmail" address (if you don't want people to show up at your home office without an appointment, get a post office box as a snailmail address, and only give clients your physical address after you've made an appointment).

- A nice addition is an "About Us" section, in which you can describe your experience, your philosophy and anything else you think will make your service attractive to clients.

Once you have created your website you want people to find it. Make sure you include your web address on your card and your brochure. You can even add it to your voice-mail message.

If you want new clients to find you, one way to get on the search engines is to go directly to each one and look for a link to submit your site. For example, if you go to Yahoo.com, at the bottom of the page you will find a link that says "How to suggest a site." You can find others at **www.searchenginewatch.com** (click on "Search Engine Listings"). Your web hosting company may offer a search engine submission service for an additional fee.

Should You Link to Retailers on Your Website?

Some retailers are happy to have you link to them on your website. But that might dilute your own business — your expertise is in rounding up exactly what your clients want so they won't have to. You don't want them to go Internet shopping by themselves, do you?

Probably not. But there's this consideration: your website is mainly a marketing tool in the strict sense of the word. You want people to call you and make appointments, not just work through your website. If they see another company's logo and a link on your website, they may erroneously think that you are promoting that company's goods over others, or that your salary comes from them. And that would make it harder for you to charge the fees you need to make this both a fun and a financially rewarding business.

So use retailers as they are used best: to buy great stuff at retail prices. Create good relationships with their sales associates so you will get help when you are looking for specific items. But don't use the retailer as a promotional avenue for your business. Most of them, even the online retailers, already have their own personal shopper of some sort.

6.3 Marketing Techniques

6.3.1 Networking Opportunities

There are different definitions of networking, but a particularly useful definition is the one given in the *American Heritage Dictionary of the English Language*:

> *"To interact or engage in informal communication with others for mutual assistance or support."*

As you will see from this definition, two keys to networking are that it is "informal" and "mutual." This type of networking does not involve making cold calls, or arranging meetings so you can talk someone into buying something. Instead, it involves meeting and interacting with people informally at social and business events.

This is where it really pays to have clearly defined your target markets. You simply do not have the time to network with "everyone" who might possibly ever have a need for a personal shopper. While some of the people you meet may have an immediate need for a personal shopper (or know someone who does), in many cases you are laying the foundation for future business. By establishing relationships through networking, you can be the one people think of when they need a personal shopper, such as when the holiday season comes around, or when they need to buy gifts for clients.

This section offers a variety of ideas, but you don't have to do all of them. Choose a few to begin with, based on your target markets. If the first ones you try don't turn out to be great networking opportunities, scratch them off your list and try something else.

Networking Clubs

Another valuable form of networking is through a networking club. Some of these are general business groups, but many have a target group of clients and include one member from different industries (e.g. insurance, financial planning, law, professional photography, real estate, etc.) to reach those in the target group. Each member of the club is expected to bring a certain number of leads to the group each week or month.

Fees will vary but can be as low as the cost of breakfast once a week or breakfast plus a membership fee. You may also be required to serve on the executive board after a time. In addition to the marketing opportunities, benefits of joining networking groups may include discounts on services provided by other members of the group.

To become a member you are either recommended to the group by an existing member, or you might approach the group and ask to sit in as an observer for a meeting or two, and get accepted from there. Most groups will allow a trial period before demanding that your join or stop coming to meetings. You may be asked to give a short presentation about your own business, and on what business and personal skills you can bring to the group.

The types of participants will differ with every group, so don't settle for the first one you visit. Check around first before deciding which one to join. Make sure the members represent the kind of very busy people with reasonable incomes who might become clients for you, or who would know others who could benefit from your services.

One way to find a networking club is through word of mouth. Ask individuals in sales jobs — such as insurance agents, financial planners, computer sales professionals, car salesmen, travel agents.

You can also look for networking groups online. Business Network International has more than 3,600 chapters in cities around the world. Find out more about the organization at **www.bni.com**.

Membership Organizations

Another excellent way to network is by joining associations that prospective clients may belong to. Some examples include:

- Civic and service clubs (such as Rotary Club or Kiwanis Club)

- Business organizations (such as your Chamber of Commerce)

- Clubs that attract the wealthy (for example, golf, polo, yachting, and country clubs)

Membership fees may vary from $20 to hundreds or even thousands of dollars (the latter if you want to join an exclusive country club or private golf club). The more expensive clubs usually require current members to introduce you and put you up for membership, so you may have to join some less exclusive clubs in order to meet people who might also belong to the more expensive clubs.

Many less exclusive clubs will let you attend a few times for a nominal fee so you can decide if you really want to join.

You can find organizations by asking your friends and colleagues what they are involved in. You can also find them in your local telephone directory or online. Here are a couple to get you started:

- *Executive Women International*
  www.executivewomen.org
  Phone: (801) 355-2800
  Fax: (801) 355-2852
  E-mail: **ewi@executivewomen.org**

- *World Chamber of Commerce Directory*
  www.chamberofcommerce.com
  Phone: (970) 663-3231
  Fax: (970) 663-6187

If you simply attend club functions without getting involved, the value of the membership will not be as great as if you truly pitch in. What sorts of things can you do to help out and gain the attention of others whose good will can help your business grow? Here are some suggestions:

- Serve on a committee

- Write articles for the association newsletter

- Volunteer to help out with the organization's events

- Run for election to the Executive Committee

Here are some additional networking tips specifically for meeting wealthy people.

Attend Openings

When a museum or art gallery has a new exhibit, they will hold an "opening" which may attract a crowd of wealthy and cultured people – often the type of people who could use shopping services.

An opening usually combines a social event, such as a wine and cheese reception, with an opportunity for people to view the exhibit. For the museum or gallery, these events can be an excellent opportunity to make sales, attract donations, or get the word out about their new exhibit. Some museums and galleries hold several openings throughout the year.

There is usually no cost or obligation to attend. In some cases, getting invited to these events can be as simple as phoning and asking to be put on the mailing list.

Another possibility is to visit local art galleries that are also dealers (retailers) and speak with the owner or manager. Explain that you are a personal shopper whose clients may be interested in purchasing art. Ask to be put on their mailing list and notified of upcoming events.

Get Involved with Charities

Many wealthy and professional people attend charitable fund-raising events such as fashion shows, teas, luncheons, dinners, etc. Attending these events yourself is one way to start connecting with the wealthy, but it can be very expensive. (Since they are "fund-raisers", getting into each event might cost you $100 or more!) Plus, there may not be much time to meet and mingle with other attendees.

You will have a much greater opportunity to connect with people and support a good cause by volunteering to help with the event. As a volunteer you may work closely with the type of people you want to attract as clients. Many wealthy people don't just make financial donations – they also donate their time to charities, and are actively involved in fund-raising and event planning.

Volunteer for activities that will bring you into contact with these people. In other words, leave the envelope stuffing to other volunteers and focus on helping out with events. In addition to serving on committees, see if you can volunteer the services of your personal shopping firm to handle donations of door prizes for the event. This will also give you an opportunity to interact with a variety of vendors. Although you will be asking for donations for the charity, many want to attract wealthy clients and you can explain how this will give them an opportunity for greater exposure.

So which charities do your target markets get involved with? If you have read *Town & Country* magazine or the social column of a local newspaper, you have probably seen photos of wealthy people at charitable events. The rich typically are involved in arts organizations, including:

- Ballet

- Theater

- Symphony

- Opera

- Visual arts

Many are also involved in health causes, such as organizations that work to find cures for AIDS or breast cancer. Others are involved with political campaigns (although technically not a "charity," political campaigns do fund-raising events where you can meet prospective clients). To volunteer, simply phone up the organizations in your community that interest you. You may be able to find them through word of mouth or listed in the Yellow Pages under a category such as "Societies" or "Charitable Organizations."

You might consider getting involved with cultural organizations, as well. Organizations formed for a single purpose, such as running your city's St. Patrick's Day Parade, are other places to find busy people who could benefit from your services.

When you choose organizations to get involved with, be sure that you have some interest in the work they do. Otherwise you will find yourself avoiding meetings and missing the chance to get involved in ways that can help both your business and the organization.

Any Group that Attracts Your Market

Whatever niche you have chosen for your personal shopping business, there will be groups of people who are most likely to use your services. If you specialize in working with seniors, for example, you could plan to join groups that most frequently attract the elderly, like chess clubs, yoga, or aquasize classes. If you target new moms and have a family yourself, then even just spending a few hours at the playground with your own kids might make some valuable connections.

If you get stuck, pick up a local newspaper and check for events happening in your area or meetings that are coming up. It shouldn't be hard to think of a group or two that will give you the chance to have casual conversations with people who are likely to use your services.

6.3.2 Promotional Events

Give a Speech

Even if you don't join an organization, you may still be able to connect with their members and get new business by being a speaker at a breakfast meeting, luncheon, or workshop.

The topic can be anything related to personal shopping that their members would be interested in. Depending on the organization, it could be anything from "Choosing a business wardrobe" to "Guidelines for corporate gift-giving." Whatever you find friends asking your advice about is probably something that many people would like to learn about.

While you probably will not be paid for your presentations, it can be an excellent opportunity to promote your business. Your company name may be published in the organization's newsletter, it will be mentioned by the person who introduces you, you can distribute business cards and brochures, and you will be able to mingle with attendees before and after your presentation. (You may get a free breakfast or lunch too!) If you give a good talk and offer useful advice, you will be seen as an expert. As long as there are people in the audience who need personal shopping services, this can be an excellent way to attract clients.

To let people know that you are available to speak, contact the local organizations mentioned above and ask friends and acquaintances if they belong to any groups that have presentations from speakers.

If you feel your speaking skills could be better, there are a couple of relatively painless ways to get comfortable talking to large groups. You can hire a speaking coach. Or you can join Toastmasters, a national organization that helps people develop their speaking skills. To find a Toastmasters chapter near you, you can check your local phone book, call their world headquarters in California at (949) 858-8255, or visit their website at **www.toastmasters.org**.

Trade Shows

As mentioned earlier, trade shows are events held in a building such as a convention center or exhibition hall, featuring booths that people can visit to learn about different products and services. These events may also be called conferences, exhibitions, fairs, special events, or simply shows.

Good promotional events for personal shoppers include shows aimed at your target market. This includes public shows such as fashion shows, women's conferences, "mom and tot" fairs, and home shows. If you are selling to the corporate market, you might consider participating in a trade show for a particular industry.

The cost to become an exhibitor (i.e. to get a booth at the show) will vary depending on the particular show, the location, the number of people expected to attend, and the amount of space you require. It may range from as little as $50 to $1,000 or more for public shows, or up to thousands of dollars for trade shows. To cut costs, you could partner with another non-competing exhibitor and share a booth space.

You can find out about upcoming shows by contacting your local convention centers, exhibition halls, or chamber of commerce. There are websites such as **www.tsnn.com** and **http://tswstg.cahners1.com/index_tsea.asp** that let you search for events by industry, type of event and location. For most events, you can then click on a link to find out contact information.

To book space as an exhibitor you will need to know how much space you require and what your needs will be. You will likely be required to sign a contract and pay a certain percentage of the cost up front. Each show will be handled differently and the show's producers should be able to tell you exactly what you need to do to book space. Many shows now have their own websites and provide registration information as well as site maps and logistical information.

Your Own Workshops or Seminars

Designing and giving your own workshops or seminars offers the double reward of promoting your business, and increasing your income on the side. Here are a few seminar ideas you might consider to promote your services:

- Holiday gift-giving ideas

- Shopping tips from a professional personal shopper

- A seminar for business men and women about dressing for business casual

- A simplify-your-life seminar which includes tips on hiring people for personal services like shopping, errands, making appointments, etc.

You will need to choose a date and time (evenings are usually best for busy people) and a location. You might approach a major retailer about holding the seminar there. Or you could book a meeting room at a hotel or conference center.

You will then have to decide how much to charge (consider making the fee comparable to continuing education courses offered in your community), or it may be free if you are offering it in conjunction with a retailer. If you are working with a retailer, they will likely market it to their customers. However, they will expect you to do some marketing yourself, and you will be responsible for getting registrations yourself if you hold it at another location.

The following is from the *FabJob Guide to Become a Motivational Speaker* which gives detailed advice on how to market a seminar:

When preparing your marketing materials, remember to focus on communicating all the benefits of attending. As well as the information, benefits of attending a seminar may include: a fun night out, a chance to network, or personal advice from an expert.

Among the other items you might include in a brochure:

- Who should attend

- When and where the seminar takes place

- How to register, including your phone number and web address

- The speaker's credentials

- Testimonials

- That enrollment is limited (mention if past seminars sold out)

- A call to action such as "Register now!"

Brochures with this information can also be used to market seminars to the public. The ideal brochure for a public seminar is one that can double as a poster (e.g. printed on one side of a colorful 8½" x 11" sheet). If permitted, try posting them at bulletin boards, especially bookstores and college campuses – two places you're likely to find people interested in seminars.

Put on a Trunk Show

Trunk shows got their name from the days when a traveling salesman would bring all his wares to town in a trunk. Today, a trunk show involves having a particular manufacturer or designer bring their product line to a location where customers can see and buy products they might not normally find at a store (e.g. a complete product line or new products).

While most trunk shows are sponsored by retail stores, you could certainly organize one yourself as a way of promoting your business. You could have the manufacturer supply the merchandise to you at wholesale prices, and then sell it at retail prices to people who attend the trunk show. Even if you don't make a ton of sales on the spot, you can provide a sign-up sheet for attendees that you can use to grow your list of clients-to-be.

You might hold a show at:

- Your own home (if it is tastefully decorated and roomy enough)

- A location you've booked, such as a meeting room at a fine hotel or restaurant

- A local retail outlet

If you have a relationship with a retailer that doesn't have staff available to organize a trunk show, you may be able to convince them to have you do the organizing, while they provide the location. However, as the store would expect to make money from the event, you might decide to do it simply to promote your services. (Of course, anything is negotiable, so you might arrange with the store to share the proceeds of the event with you.)

In addition to finding a place for the event, you will need to find a designer or manufacturer to participate. You can track down someone you would like to work with through the resources mentioned elsewhere in this guide (e.g. the Resources section or section 3.2 on Vendors). Since major manufacturers and designers may not be available, consider working with an "up and comer" – a young designer or new manufacturer that isn't yet as well established. They will likely be more eager to participate. You might even convince the designer to make a personal appearance at the event.

You will then need to market the event. If you're holding it at a retailer, they should have a list of customers to invite. Otherwise, you will need to invite your own clients, and promote the event through advertising and publicity (covered below) as well as networking.

You may get some ideas from observing what retailers do to promote their events. Here's an example from an article in *Lustre* magazine, published at JewelersResources.com, which describes what was done for an event at Brinsmaids, a suburban Connecticut jewelry store:

"Owner Scott Cusson sent formal printed invitations to prospec-tive buyers, placed ads in the local newspaper and posted signs

in the store announcing the event. The store remained open several extra hours for a cocktail reception with hors d'oeuvres, champagne and wine. And finally, he earmarked a portion of all trunk show sales for the local chapter of the American Red Cross."

6.3.3 Advertising

Yellow Pages

You have probably used the Yellow Pages many times to find things you're interested in. But before you buy an ad for your own business, you should carefully investigate the costs compared to the potential return.

Many new business owners find a Yellow Pages ad does not make the phone ring off the hook with buyers. If someone does respond to your ad, they may be "shopping around" so you must be prepared to invest time as well as advertising dollars if you use this method of advertising.

To minimize your risk, you might want to consider starting with a small word ad or a small display ad such as 1/8 page. If you can get your hands on a previous year's edition of your local Yellow Pages, compare the ads for personal shoppers from year to year. If you notice others have increased or decreased the size of their ads, this can give you an indication of what might work for you.

You can either design the ad yourself, have the Yellow Pages design it for you, or hire a designer. Take a look at the ads in your current Yellow Pages for ideas. (The category will vary depending on the city. Try looking under Shopping Services if you don't find ads listed under Personal Shoppers). If you are interested in advertising, contact your local Yellow Pages to speak with a sales rep.

Some localities also have "pages" or "books" of other types. In the mid-Atlantic states, the community Yellow Pages are alternatives. These are limited to smaller geographic areas than, for example, a whole state or city. Check into that possibility, as well, especially if you don't want to travel great distances to find clients.

Magazine and Newspaper Advertising

Advertising can be expensive, and may not generate the results you want unless you do it repeatedly. (It has been estimated that many people need to see an advertisement three to seven times before they buy.) Therefore, if you choose to buy advertising, it will probably be most cost effective to place ads in local magazines or newspapers aimed at your target market.

For example, if you specialize in working with busy moms, you can advertise in local parenting magazines. If you live in a big city or one of its suburbs, your region probably has a publication like *Baltimore's Child*, a monthly devoted to everything local for parents and children. This type of advertising is affordable, and word of mouth also works well for those who have advertised in it just a few times.

You can also make arrangements with other businesses (photographers, exercise programs, etc.) that advertise to promote each other's businesses to the clients you currently have. This is called strategic partnering and is a great way to increase your client base through referrals.

Be aware of the seasons in your business. If you're in apparel consulting, you'll have four seasons, plus the winter holidays, to take advantage of people's need to revamp and expand their wardrobes. If you are in gifts, the winter holidays are your biggest opportunity to grow your business. But don't forget graduation time and other "calendar days" (Administrative Assistants' Day, Boss's Day, etc.) to promote your gift services.

Sometimes, local newspapers and magazines run special promotions and special sections at these times. But remember to plan ahead. Magazines generally work at least three months ahead in planning their issues and the advertising they will accept for those issues. So think Christmas in July, summer at the end of winter and so on.

But if you're in a fashion-oriented niche of personal shopping, you'll be that far ahead anyway, as that's when you'll have to investigate new items coming from designers and manufacturers for the upcoming season.

Here are some tips for effective advertising:

- Make your ad about your customers. Explain how they can benefit from your services rather than just listing the services you provide. (Saying "You can have the wardrobe you've always wanted" is better than saying "I help people expand their wardrobes.")

- Make them an offer they can't refuse. Your ad should describe a service or special promotion that makes you stand out from your competition. It should also include a call to action (i.e. saying "Call today" or including a coupon that expires by a certain date).

- Make sure you're available for people who respond to your ad. If someone wants to talk to you but keeps getting your voice-mail, they may give up.

- Make long-term plans for your advertising program. Chances are that running an ad only once won't give you as much business as you would hope. Develop a long-term advertising strategy and stick with it.

The publications you advertise in will usually design your ad for an additional cost and give you a copy of the ad to run in other publications.

However, you will get much better results if you can manage to get free publicity in those publications, instead of paying for advertising.

6.3.4 Free Publicity

When a business gets publicity in a magazine article, newspaper story, radio or television talk show, it can result in a tremendous amount of new business. Here are some ways personal shoppers can get publicity.

Press Releases

A press release is a brief document that you submit to the media in order to gain publicity for your business. Editors prefer to see a press release as a single page (under 500 words) and written as if it were a news story. But don't expect it to be run "as is." Most editors will rewrite your press release slightly to fit their standards.

Here are some tips for writing a good press release:

- Make sure the press release is newsworthy. For example, you could write about an upcoming event you'll be speaking at.

- Give your press release a strong lead paragraph that answers the six main questions: who, what, where, when, why, and how.

- Include factual information about yourself and your services. Remember, a press release should read like a news story, not an advertisement.

- Keep it short. Aim for a maximum of 500 words.

- Include your contact information at the end of the press release so that reporters and readers can get ahold of you.

You can find numerous online resources to help you write a press release, including **www.publicityinsider.com/release.asp**.

Most magazines and newspapers publish contact information for their editors. Newspapers may have dozens of editors, so make sure you send your submission to the appropriate one. For example, you would probably want to contact the Business Editor for your new business announcement, and the Lifestyle Editor if your specialty is doing personal shopping for seniors.

As an alternative to writing a press release, you could call the editor or send him or her a brief "pitch letter" to suggest an idea for a story. If you want a few pointers on writing pitch letters, try going to **www. publicityinsider.com/pitch.asp**.

Make your pitch letter as interesting as possible. Many publications will print brief information, but it's hard to get them to print anything longer. To do that, you'll have to provide a hook — the element of your story that will be of interest to readers. For example, you might suggest that the publication do a story about how your help putting together a basic wardrobe for a mom getting off welfare changed her life.

TIP: Donating your time and expertise to charities and getting retailers to kick in some merchandise can be a great promotional idea for all concerned. Plus, you'll help out someone who needs and deserves help. Don't get involved in civic programs simply to promote your business. However, don't ignore the option, either, especially as your example might inspire others to help out.

While it is not necessary to submit photographs to a daily newspaper editor (most newspapers have their own photographers), photographs may help attract the editor's attention. They might also be published in a smaller magazine, newspaper or newsletter that doesn't have a photographer on staff. If you send photos, remember to make sure you have signed model releases from the people in the photos as well as the photographer (see section 6.2.2). Put the photos in an attractive two-pocket folder with your business card and a cover letter. Then follow up a week later with a phone call.

Write an Article or Column

One of the best ways to establish yourself as an expert is to write articles or a column for a newspaper, magazine, or newsletter. While it can be tough to break into large daily newspapers, there may be an opportunity to write for smaller newspapers or local magazines.

You could write on any topic related to shopping (e.g. tips for buying wedding presents, how to spot a bargain, tips for buying a new bathing suit), or you could volunteer to answer reader questions. The length and frequency of your column will depend on the publication's needs. You might produce a weekly 500-word column for a local newspaper, or a monthly 1,000-word column for a newsletter or magazine.

Remember to give your readers real information. This won't detract from the value of your services at all. Those who use the information and never call you would never call you anyway. Those who call you will do so because you enticed them — you gave away a little of what you know, and showed them how much more you could do.

You will probably have to write the first column or article and show it to the editor; unless you are an experienced and published writer, they won't say yes to you unless they see what you're selling. If you don't immediately offer to do it for free, you might even get paid for it. But do be careful not to make it an advertisement for yourself, regardless of whether you get paid. The short bio most publications run with non-staff stories will tell the readers what you want them to know — how to get in touch with you to hire your expert assistance.

Television and Radio Talk Shows

If you've always wanted to be an on-air personality, here's your chance. The best shows for personal shoppers to appear on are morning and afternoon talk shows, and sometimes, depending on your specialty, business shows or business segments of news shows. Phone the appropriate producer at the local stations and let them know that you would be happy to appear and provide your expertise for their audience.

You will probably be asked to send some information; this is where your promotional materials come in handy. After you've sent them or dropped them off, give the producer a couple of days to look them over and ask for an appointment. Producers are often bombarded with local folks who think they have something to say, so be sure to use your best "hooks" to grab the producer's attention.

6.4 Marketing to Corporate Clients

Whether you're looking to work with major corporations or up-and-coming entrepreneurs, working with corporate clients can be fun, exciting, and financially rewarding. Many of the techniques already mentioned in this chapter can help you break into the corporate market.

For example, clients may hire you after meeting you at networking events, hearing you give a speech, or reading about you in the newspaper. However, you don't have to wait for clients to call you. Instead, you can take the initiative and contact prospective clients. In this section you will learn how to take the initiative and break into this lucrative market.

6.4.1 Your Warm Market

Your "warm market" is anyone who knows you. It includes friends, family members, neighbors, former co-workers, members of organizations you belong to, and anyone else you know. These are people that you already have a relationship with. If you phone them, you know they will return the call.

Chances are, your warm market includes a number of people who are "decision-makers" in an organization that could use your services. In other words, they are in a position where they could hire your company. If not, they may be able to recommend your services to the decision-maker. But even before getting the corporation on board as a client, you may find a number of individuals in your warm market who can use your services.

That's essentially how Ilene Mackler became a personal shopper with a very lucrative niche. Mackler was a suburban Baltimore new mom when she decided, in 1990, that she wanted to do two things: bring more money into the household and stay home with her daughter full-time..

> "I didn't want a job where I had to spend 80 percent of my income to pay for live-in help, nor did I want live-in help to raise my child. My husband is in sales, and every year, for the holidays, he has to find gifts for his clients. I often did it. Finally he said to me, 'You know, I bet a lot of businesspeople send their husband, wife, boy-friend, or girlfriend to the mall. They would love someone to come to the office. They could explain that they need to spend $50 for a gift for each client, and they'd like to see some choices.'
>
> I said, 'OK, I can do that.' So I did a little research and went to my first trade show in New York City, armed with information I had looked up about corporate gifts ahead of time. When I got back, I called on friends who were businesspeople. Lo and behold, at Christmas time, I had orders. After that, the same people who had ordered for Christmas called and said, for instance, that they had to go to a conference and needed some giveaways. I said, 'I can do that.'
>
> Later on, someone else called and asked if I did gift baskets. I say, 'Yes, I can do that.' One request has led to another. While a great deal of my business is in wearables such as Bobby Jones golf shirts for executives, awards for golf outing winners, govern-ment event items and so on, it has also taken me on some inter-esting roads.

I got the opportunity to commission artwork for a client's office, and I've done things for the Preakness, one of the top three racing events in the country. This has taken us on so many interesting roads through life."

Ilene Mackler now owns Power Presents, which works with major corporate clients such as Estée Lauder, Motorola and the U.S. Office of the Secretary of Defense. She got her start by picking up the phone and calling people she knew. You could do the same. However, even though you will be contacting people you know, it's important to remember that you are calling about a business matter. While you may get the odd project purely on the basis of your relationship with someone (for example, your dad may hire you to buy holiday gifts for his clients just because he loves you), in most cases in order to get hired you will need to communicate the value you will bring to the company.

In the next section you will find some advice on what to say when calling prospective clients that you don't know. Notice the wording used to convey the value of hiring a personal shopper, and incorporate it into your communication with your warm market.

6.4.2 Cold Calling

Cold calling involves picking up the telephone and calling strangers. It is something many people fear doing. But it can be an effective way of generating business for those who are confident and not too afraid of hearing the word "no."

Because the reality is that some people will say "no." Some will not even give you the opportunity to say why you are calling. However, it is also a reality that there are people who need personal shopping services who don't know where to turn – and would welcome a call from someone who can help them.

For example, if you specialize in corporate gift-giving, chances are that there are people in your community right now who need to get gifts for clients but feel overwhelmed with the task and wish someone could handle it for them. You are offering something these people need and want. With that in mind, look at each call as simply an introduction of your services – services that could possibly help this person and organization.

Here's a short course in cold-calling that you can use no matter what corporate market you choose.

Finding Contact Information

The first step in making cold calls is to have a list of companies to call. The obvious way to get phone numbers is by picking up the Yellow Pages and choosing companies in industries you'd like to work with. However, the Yellow Pages won't give you a contact name.

For more detailed information about companies in your community, you can call your local Chamber of Commerce to see if you can get a list of their members. Some chambers will only give the list to other members. In which case you may either decide to join the Chamber of Commerce (if you haven't done so already), or buy the list.

Another alternative is to find the membership list at your local public library. The central library in your city will very likely have numerous business directories, including one or more directories with contact information for local businesses. This information may be broken down by industry and company size.

Once you've decided on the companies you'd like to solicit, you'll need to identify the best person to speak with, the decision-maker. Depending on your specialization and the size of the company, there may actually be several people in the organization that could use your services.
For example, any of the following departments might use the services of a personal shopper or concierge business:

- CEO or President

- Human Resources

- Marketing

- Public Relations

- Purchasing

- Sales

You could call to introduce your services to decision-makers in each of these departments. (In many large organizations, the key decision-maker in each department has the title of Vice-President or Department Head.) On the other hand, if the company is small, there may be a single individual you should talk to, such as an owner or office manager.

If you don't have the name of a decision-maker when you call a company, simply ask the receptionist. You might ask: "Can you tell me the name of the person who buys the gifts your company gives to its clients?" Or you might ask: "What is the name of the Vice-President in charge of Marketing?"

When you get a name from a receptionist, make sure you ask for the correct spelling and the correct extension or direct line. If the name could belong either to a male or female (like Tracy, Chris, or Pat), also ask if the person is a man or a woman.

If you have asked who buys corporate gifts, and the receptionist doesn't know, ask for the assistant to the CEO, or the marketing department. They are likely to know who buys gifts (one of them may actually be in charge of it).

If the receptionist puts you through to an assistant in the decision-maker's department, you can go through the same procedure of asking for the decision-maker's name and direct phone number.

Be prepared, however, that the assistant may be a "gatekeeper." In other words, it may be the assistant's job to screen out calls from anyone the decision-maker doesn't know. While this certainly won't happen every time, it is something to prepare for. Remember that this person has a great deal of power over whether you ever get an appointment with the decision-maker. So do not try to bully the assistant.

If he or she says, "Just send us your information," politely explain that while you will be happy to do that, you want to make sure the information addresses the company's needs and would like just a couple of minutes to check those out with the decision-maker. Then ask the assistant to advise you about the best time to call the decision-maker.

The sections that follow this one offer some suggested alternatives in the event that you are not able to get through to the decision-maker on the telephone. However, let's assume that you will be put through to the decision-maker. Now you need to know what to say.

What to Say (and What Not to Say)

It would be great if you could just strike up a spontaneous conversation with a prospective client and convince them to hire you.

However, most people who are starting out don't find it easy to say the right things off the top of their head. So it's a good idea to have scripts for leaving a message on voicemail as well as for your first conversation with a potential client. A script is simply an outline of what you want to say during your call. It helps you clearly communicate the main points you want to get across.

Be prepared for the fact that many decision-makers screen their calls with voice mail. They simply don't have time to speak with everyone who wants their attention. Whether or not they return your call depends primarily on how intriguing your message is. First, here's an example of what not to say:

> "Um, hi. My name is Sharon Shopper. I'm a personal shopper. Well, actually, I'm just beginning my career as a personal shopper, mainly for corporate gifts because I know they're always in demand and my family really needs the money I can make from this.
>
> Anyway, I used to work in customer service at a tire store so I'm sure your company can benefit from my service-orientation and the fact that if I can deal with irate customers in a tire store, I can sure work with corporate managers about gifts. People like gifts a whole lot more than buying tires..."

Get the picture? This personal shopper wouldn't get a call back. Here are some major mistakes the caller made:

Saying, "I'm Just a Beginner"

It is hard to think of an instance where you would want to volunteer the fact that you are a beginner. After all, how would you feel about your brain surgeon if he said he was "just a beginner"? Don't see yourself as a rookie, but as an idea person who has the experience and expertise to make things happen for potential clients.

Talking About "Me, Me, Me"

Notice how many times the caller said "I" or "me." Potential clients, like most other humans, are more interested in their own needs than hearing "me-focused" comments like these.

Burdening Your Potential Client With Your Survival

"My family really needs the money I can make from this" is not an appropriate thing to say to a prospective client. You don't want pity. You want to run a business. You want to serve clients. Tell them what you can do for them, not what you want them to do for you. See yourself as a businessperson exploring whether doing business with this company would be beneficial for both of you.

Communicate your message with confidence. Assume that what you offer is something the decision-maker wants. Assume you can do, with excellence, anything your clients want. Your call is much more likely to be returned if that can-do attitude infects every contact you make with every potential client on the planet.

Instead, here's a much better approach, which can be modified to suit whatever your own specialization is.

> "Hello (first name of potential client), this is Sharon Shopper. I offer services that companies can use to enhance their customer and employee recognition programs, and save managers time as well. I'm a specialist in finding unique business gifts at great prices, and getting them delivered any way you want. When would you have a few minutes for me to show you my portfolio of gifts I've arranged for other companies?"

Or you might simply say:

"Hello, Mr. O'Busy. This is Sharon Shopper. I help companies improve their relationships with their clients and employees by finding unique business gifts at great prices. Please give me a call at 555-1234 so we can discuss how this service would benefit your company."

Superstar speaker Mark Victor Hansen reports that when he used to call prospective employers, he would leave a message simply stating his name, phone number, and the message, "It's good news." In many cases he found his message was intriguing enough to get people to call back. When a prospective employer returned the call, his "good news" was that he was available to work for them. You probably won't be able to do that. But you could include a line such as, "I have a great gift for you." And you could offer a ten-percent discount certificate for an initial order, or something of value that you are willing to give to the prospect whether you make a sale or not.

If your call is intriguing and the company needs gift-buying services or is looking to improve its business relationships – as many companies are – your call is likely to get returned. However, there is no way to get appointments with every single person you call, not even if you are Julia Roberts. (Well, unless you say you're from the IRS and have a "serious matter" to discuss.)

But failing either of those two things, just be polite and move on when you don't get the response you're seeking. Remember, there is a buyer for every product and service. People bought Pet Rocks, for goodness' sake! And you are offering something that is a thousand times better than that. (Although if a client wanted to send her own customers Pet Rocks, you'd find them, wouldn't you? Or have them made. See more on that in section 3.2 on finding vendors.)

How Often Should You Call?

While a few decision-makers say that persistence pays off (in other words, someone who calls repeatedly will eventually get their call returned), they are probably the exception to the rule. Most decision-makers say someone who pesters them turns them off. One woman mentioned that she makes a mental note of the people who call repeatedly and resolves never to have anything to do with them.

Calling without leaving a message may seem like a good idea, but many business-people have caller ID on their telephone. If they see a dozen calls from someone who doesn't leave a message, they are likely to assume the caller is selling something they would not be interested in. Not only will the decision-maker not pick up the phone, but also they may become so irritated with the calls that they may respond negatively when the caller finally does leave a message.

If your first call is not returned, call a second time a few days later, just in case your first message didn't get through. Messages are rarely erased accidentally, but you wouldn't want to miss a business opportunity if, for some reason, it happened to your call. If neither of your calls is returned, it may be wise to wait awhile before calling again or focus instead on prospective clients who are interested in working with you.

> **TIP:** You are much more likely to get your call returned if you say you were referred by someone the decision-maker knows and respects. Ask for referrals from all your clients and slip "_____ suggested I call you" into the script after your name.

Once You Get Through to the Decision-Maker

Many of the same principles for leaving a message apply when you are speaking directly with the decision-maker. For these calls, you should prepare and practice a script that works well for you. The following is the type of script that has proven to be very effective. If the decision-maker answers the phone, assume he or she is willing to talk, and launch right into your script:

> **YOU:** Hello (first name of potential employer), this is Sharon Shopper. I'm calling about a service that can enhance your client relations, and save your company time and money as well.

> **TIP:** Unless you have already met the person you are calling, avoid starting your conversation with pleasantries like, "How are you today?" before stating your name and why you are calling. Using pleasantries with a stranger is often associated with people calling to "sell" something and may create suspicion.

YOU: *(Say lightly, as if the answer is obviously "yes")* I'm sure you would say maintaining great client relations is something (insert name of potential employer's company) cares about, isn't it? And saving money could make it that much better.

TIP: The decision-maker will respond at this point. Most should respond positively. If he or she doesn't respond positively, you may want to cut the call short and move on to the next name on your list. Trying to turn someone around who won't respond politely to even the most basic question is almost always a waste of time and energy.

YOU: I thought so. My services can help (insert name of company) increase client satisfaction and create more repeat business. I'm a specialist in finding unique business gifts at great prices, and getting them delivered any way you want. I have a 15-minute presentation that explains my services in detail. I'd like to meet with you to show you my portfolio of gifts I've arranged for other companies. Do you have 15 minutes in your schedule on Wednesday afternoon, or might Thursday morning work better for you?

As the example above illustrates, you can avoid a mistake many cold callers make of giving the decision-maker a choice between saying "yes" to a meeting or saying "no."

Instead, give them a choice between two possible meeting dates. If you want to set up a meeting, you should also clearly state a time limit – ideally no more than 20 minutes –because many decision-makers view their time as limited.

You may get a nibble right then, and an appointment. Or the decision-maker may ask you to send things to look at before you're offered an appointment. If that's the case, say:

"I'll be happy to do that. If you can switch me back to your assistant, I'll make sure I have the proper mailing information. And if I may, I'll just touch base with you around the middle of next week. Thanks so much, Mr. O'Busy."

However, instead of getting an appointment or an invitation to send something, don't be surprised to get at least a mild objection. An excellent way to respond is to agree with how the decision-maker feels and explain that many other people felt exactly the same way until they had a chance to learn more about your program.

CLIENT: We don't have a need for this type of program right now.

YOU: I understand how you feel. Many of my clients felt exactly the same way until I was able to show them how they could benefit from this service. I'd like to show you the same thing. Would Wednesday afternoon work for you, or would Thursday morning be better?

Although you are not giving them any more information, the above statement can be surprisingly effective in getting the client to agree to a meeting. Often the first objection is an automatic reaction, and just a little push can get you in the door. However, if the client wants more information, you can certainly give them more. For example,

CLIENT: We always want to save some money and maintain good client relations, but I'd have to know a little bit more about what you're selling to set up an appointment.

YOU: I understand. In addition to showing you how to give memorable gifts that can help you get more business from your clients, I can show you how to improve employee loyalty through something as simple as a small gift. Would Wednesday afternoon work for you, or would Thursday morning be better?

If the decision-maker is still not interested, then move on to the next person on your list. If you are overly aggressive, most decision-makers will be turned off and may not want to do business with you even if they hear good things about you from another source. Your time could be better spent focusing on people who are interested in what you have to offer.

Don't worry if your first few calls don't go as planned. Consider them practice. Once you have been using this approach for a while, it should generate a respectable success rate. Depending on what you are proposing (business gifts, concierge services, etc.), a good success rate for setting up meetings may be one "yes" out of every ten calls or even one "yes" out of every two calls. It is up to you to determine if making a lot of cold calls is a good use of your time.

If this approach doesn't work, go back and take a hard look at your script. Are you clearly communicating the benefits of taking the action you suggest to the decision-maker? If you believe you are, ask someone you respect to listen to you make some of your calls. They may discover something in the way you communicate that could be improved.

Having Someone Phone For You

An alternative to phoning yourself is to have someone phone for you. This can give the impression that you are already an established corporate consulting firm. Like many of us, clients can be influenced by how things appear, and may assume you are a successful professional to have people working for you.

One way to have someone call for you is to hire someone you pay on an hourly or commission basis. This person might work for you full-time or part-time, from your office or from their home. You might find the right person through word of mouth or from a classified ad. In addition to phoning, you might have the person you hire assist you with other tasks as well. (Chapter 5 has more information on hiring employees and contractors.)

Another alternative is to have a friend or relative call on your behalf. Ideally this person should have a different last name from yours, or they should simply introduce themselves by their first name. (It doesn't sound nearly as impressive to hear, "Hello, this is Shawn Shopper calling on behalf of Sharon Shopper.")

6.5 Working With Clients

No matter what marketing techniques you use, you can expect to start getting calls from people interested in using your services. In this section you will find some tips for working with prospective clients and turning them into paying clients.

6.5.1 First Phone Call

Your first contact with new clients will probably be over the phone, when they call to ask about your services and prices. Have a full packet of your promotional materials on your desk near the phone so you can refer to them, and be sure you don't leave anything out.

Also, write down the caller's phone number and address, too, if possible. Then you'll have it and you'll be able to enter it into your database if the caller becomes a customer. And you'll also have it if the caller doesn't immediately become a customer. Enter it into your database with other prospects and e-mail them from time to time. Let them know about special events they might be interested in, or about things you discovered in the initial conversation that might make them become clients later on.

For example, a caller may say he is investigating the possibility of a gift for all the children attending his upcoming wedding, which is seven months away. He wants to do this without involving the bride or the wedding planner. The conversation ends with him saying he wants to think about it a little more. In your database, his name should pop up in about a month, reminding you to make contact with him. If you're wise, you will have done a little research, even without knowing more about his situation, so he can see that you are interested and diligent. And, of course, it gives you a good reason to make contact.

Most callers will also want to know how much you charge for your services. As soon as you've told them a number, resell them on the idea — tell them again how your services will make a great difference in their appearance, their lifestyle, and so on.

Your main effort in an initial telephone inquiry, however, is to get the potential client to make an appointment to fully discuss his or her needs and desires. There is still no guarantee that you'll get a client or a project, but if they are willing to spend their valuable time seeing you – and time is usually what your clients have little of – chances are very good that they will become a client.

An initial conversation might sound like the following. This gives a good example of how to sell a client on your fee.

YOU: Good morning. Sharon Shopper, at your service. What can we do for you today?

CLIENT: I was wondering if you could help me with my wardrobe. I'm feeling a little dated, and I need to look sharp if I ever want to move up in this business.

YOU: What business is that?

CLIENT: I work for a record company.

YOU: Oh, yes, in that segment of the entertainment industry, you definitely need to look trendy.

CLIENT: What do you charge?

YOU: We have several ways to arrange our fees. We can spend half a day with you going through your wardrobe and recommending supplementary purchases. Then, of course, we can make those purchases for you if time is a real issue. Or we can work by the project, for instance, if you only need a new outfit for job-hunting.

CLIENT: But how many dollars? I'm not at the top of my pay scale yet.

YOU: Our half-day service is $250, and then we generally add ten percent to the price of garments and accessories we purchase. But think of it this way: we don't charge for our initial consultation, and our work will save you so much. You won't buy clothes that don't work, or that don't hang right on you. We save you from having to return items, or even from having to live with them if they are not return- able.

    A half day once or twice a year more than pays for itself just in costs on clothing. It does better than that when you add in the improvement in your image and your self-con- fidence. When is a convenient time for us to meet and discuss what you might like us to do for you?

CLIENT: I'm not sure... but...

YOU: There is no charge for our initial meeting, and you can make up your mind then. Should we meet early next week? Maybe at your office?

CLIENT: Yes, could we meet at my office at lunchtime on Wednesday?

YOU: Certainly.

And then you would get her office address, cell phone number and so on. And mark it in your calendar, with a note to confirm the appointment the day before.

6.5.2 First Meeting

What to Bring to the Meeting

Most importantly, you need to bring your curiosity and your expertise... but those you carry in your head. In your briefcase, you will need:

- A notepad and questionnaire you've developed to obtain all the information you need about the client's desires, preferences, sizes and so on. (Sample questionnaires can be found on the CD-ROM that comes with this book.)

- Your presentation portfolio

- Business cards

- Additional photos of your work for other clients

- Brochures from vendors whose merchandise you think would particularly suit this client

- Your calendar for a year ahead

- A small calculator

- Blank contracts

- Forms for processing credit-card payments for the fee for the client's consulting session (if applicable)

How to Dress

Even if your niche is corporate gifts, you still need to look up-to-date. If your niche is very trendy clothes for very young women, and you're not so young, you'll have to look trendy.

Your first impression will last, especially because of the business you're in. So whatever style you choose, make sure that everything you wear fits perfectly, that your shoes are in good repair and shined, that your makeup is the most flattering it can be (ditto for hair) and that you do not overpower the client with scent. Light, clean scents – and definitely not the "stinker" scents that actually make some people gag – are best. Don't use any if you're in doubt.

Stay away from looks that are too casual. Even if your specialty is arranging Hawaiian sabbaticals for professors who love to surf, you need to dress for business. You are buying a whole lifestyle for this person.

While the client can look as if she is going to spend six months in Lanai, you cannot. If she wanted a beach bum to do the planning and shopping for her, she'd have done it herself!

But don't be boring. Even if your clients are very professional, you are in a creative business. So add a funky piece of jewelry or a designer hand-bag to set off your outfit.

Men who are personal shoppers for a big retail corporation will wear suits, slacks, and blazers. But those with their own personal shopping business can choose suits/blazers or business casual, depending on their specialty and clientele. For example, if you are a personal shopper for business gifts and trips, you'd wear a suit to meet clients.

Developing a Client Relationship

The fact that this busy person has agreed to meet with you means they are interested in your services. As mentioned above, while there is no guarantee that you will get a particular client or project, chances are good that if they have a need for your services and are meeting with you, they will become a client.

This is where your knowledge of relationship selling will really pay off (see section 2.3.1 if this is an area you need to improve). You can begin by giving a quick overview of your services, however, during your meet-ing you should mostly ask and listen. Aim to have your client do about 80% of the talking. (Of course take your cue from the client. If they prefer not to do a lot of talking, don't try to force it.)

Your purpose during this meeting is to turn a prospective client into a client. The way to do this is by identifying what your client needs and wants, so you can communicate how your services will benefit them. Do they want to:

- Free up their time for more important things?

- Avoid making mistakes when buying gifts?

- Start dressing like an executive before applying for a promotion?

- Improve their image to get back into the dating scene?

- Give their home a makeover?

Each client will have unique needs or problems for which you can provide solutions. For example, a small business may be losing employees, or a husband may have disappointed his wife with previous gifts.

The prospective client may not tell you exactly what their problems are, but they will often tell you what they do want. The small business may think he could attract top job applicants if he offered a concierge service as an employee benefit, or the husband may want to ensure his wife is delighted on their anniversary.

In addition to learning what the prospective client wants out of your services in general, your first meeting is an opportunity to get specific information. To do so, you should have a questionnaire that you can fill out during your initial consultation. (You can use the questionnaires on the CD-ROM, or refer to section 3.1.1 to see sample questions.)

Why should you fill out the questionnaire, and not them? Because by conversing with them, you will bring out details that might not be revealed otherwise. For example, if a woman says her dress size is 10, she might not mention that she wears an 8 when it comes to designer clothes. If you ask the question and she answers, "Ten," you can ask, "All the time? Or are there some designers whose clothes fit you better in a smaller or larger size?" Think of as many questions as you need to give you the best, most thorough profile possible.

Knowing the details will save you time later and help you serve each client better. Don't count on keeping all of it in your head; count on keeping it on these forms and spending a little time updating them if clients need to make any changes.

Once you have filled out the questionnaire, the next step is to get the client to sign a contract. A couple of samples are included in the next section. Finally, you will need to get the credit information required to make purchases (as discussed in section 5.4.5).

A Final Note

No matter how your meeting goes – whether you end up with a client or not – a thank-you note is important. If the meeting did result in a client, you need to thank the person for that. If it didn't, you need to thank the person for his or her time, and be sure to tell them you are available to serve them when they do decide to shift the burden of image and shopping to you. Plus, even if they are not ready, it gives them a chance to mention to their friends who need a personal shopper: "Hey, I know someone you could hire ..."

7. Resources

In this section of the guide you will find a variety of resources – magazines, websites and professional organizations that can help you keep up with current trends and learn more about the areas you want to specialize in as a personal shopper.

There are thousands of resources in the areas of fashion, gifts, and other areas of interest to personal shoppers. To make your job easier, we have reviewed the overwhelming number of choices, and compiled a list of top resources to give you a place to get started.

7.1 Fashion Resources

Websites

The Internet has more than 14 million websites that cover the topic of fashion. We've narrowed down the list to a few of the best sites for keeping on top of fashion trends and industry news. (Websites for fashion magazines are listed below.)

- *Fashion.net*
  www.fashion.net

- *FashionInformation.com*
  www.fashioninformation.com

- *Fashionlines*
  www.fashionlines.com

- *Fashion Planet*
  www.fashion-planet.com

- *Fashion Wire Daily*
  www.fashionwiredaily.com/headlines.weml

- *Fashion U.K.*
  www.fuk.co.uk

- *Hint Magazine*
  www.hintmag.com

- *The New York Times: Fashion & Style*
  www.nytimes.com/pages/fashion

Trade Publications

The following magazines are read by people who work as professionals in the fashion and retail industries.

- *Apparel Magazine*
  News stories about the apparel industry.
  www.apparelmag.com

- *ApparelNews.net*
  News and features from the apparel industry.
  www.apparelnews.net

- *Children's Business*
  Retail and style information about children's wear.
  www.childrensbusiness.com

- *DNR*
  DNR is the leading news magazine of men's fashion and retail.
  www.dailynewsrecord.com

- *Look Online*
  A \$59 subscription to Look Online's *Daily Fashion Report* includes lots of goodies such as the *New York Fashion Events Schedule*, the "A" list of the most important fashion related shows, parties, store openings, and charity events going on in New York City for the upcoming two week period.
  www.lookonline.com/membernew.html

- *Women's Wear Daily (WWD)*
  WWD is considered the leading source for women's fashion news. A subscription to the online version costs \$99 per year.
  www.wwd.com

- *Worth Global Style Network*
  www.wgsn.com/public

Consumer Magazines

The following are among the best of the consumer magazines (i.e. for the general public). Your customers will be reading these magazines, so it's a good idea to keep up with what they cover. Websites are given for each publication, although they can also be found on the newsstand or your public library, or ordered by subscription.

- *Elle*
  www.elle.com

- *Flare (Canada)*
  www.flare.com

- *Harper's Bazaar*
  www.harpersbazaar.com

- *Style.com (W and Vogue)*
  www.style.com

- *Vogue U.K.*
  http://vogue.co.uk

Organizations

- *Fashion Group International*
  Members represent all areas of the fashion, apparel, accessories, beauty and home industries. You can qualify for membership once you have at least three years of experience in a professional or managerial position in a fashion related industry.
  www.fgi.org/home.html

- *Association of Image Consultants International*
  A professional association for anyone working in fashion or image consulting. Provides a variety of services, including a mentor program and magazine. Membership costs $249 per year.
  www.aici.org

7.2   Resources for Other Specializations

There are hundreds of publications covering areas a personal shopper might specialize in. We have included a selection of top resources as a starting point. If you are particularly interested in one of these areas, you will be able to find many other publications at your local library or news stand.

Gifts

- *Gift Association of America*
  This association is mainly aimed at the needs of gift buyers but useful to other niches as well. Membership costs $115 per year and offers many benefits, including a useful membership directory (good for finding local sources of items), plus discounts on shipping and other products and services.
  www.giftassoc.org

- *Gift Basket Review*
  The latest trends in gift baskets plus tips on selling to corporate clients.
  www.festivities-pub.com

- *Gifts and Decorative Accessories*
  A trade magazine for the retail gift industry.
  www.giftsanddec.com

- *Gifts and Magazines*
  A website with dozens of categories of gifts. The selection of vendors is limited, and you will have to scroll past ads, but it may spark some ideas.
  www.giftsandmagazines.com/links/GiftIdeaLinks.html

- *Retail News*
  A trade magazine published by the Canadian Gift & Tableware Association. The website includes articles and a list of upcoming giftware trade shows throughout North America.
  www.cgta.org/cgta_retailnews_home.asp

- *Toy Directory*
  This website lists virtually all the toy wholesalers in the U.S. It includes toy recalls and plenty of marketing information, including forecasts of what's going to be hot next season. You can also request catalogs so you can have a handy guide to virtually all the toys on the market — even if you end up buying them at retail.
  www.toydirectory.com

- *Wholesale Source Magazine*
  A trade magazine for the general merchandise and gift industry.
  http://wsmag.com/subscription.html

- *UK Gifts Guide*
  This U.K. website has links to gift sites for a number of categories. Includes some unique gift ideas.
  www.ukgiftsguide.co.uk

Food and Wine

- *Epicurious.com*
  An electronic publication with some of the best articles from *Bon Appétit* and *Gourmet*, two consumer magazines that your food-loving clients are reading (and that you can find on news stands).
  http://www.epicurious.com

- *Foodsupplier.com ezine*
  An online trade publication with information about gourmet foods and food suppliers.
  www.foodsupplier.com

- *Wine Enthusiast*
  Includes information about corporate gifts.
  www.wineenthusiast.com

- *Wine Spectator*
  Solid information on global wines plus trends, dining and lifestyle features.
  www.winespectator.com

TIP: In some states, a personal shopper cannot actually buy the wine to be included as gifts, but they can advise clients on wines to buy. Usually it is fine if the customer has purchased wine for the personal shopper to add it to other items in a gift package. Check this in your own jurisdiction.

Home Furnishings and Accessories

In addition to the publications listed below, check your local news stand for consumer magazines such as *Elle Decor*, *House Beautiful*, and *House & Garden*. Your clients will be reading these magazines along with any local home decorating magazines (such as *Atlanta Homes & Lifestyles*, *Florida Design*, *Seattle Homes & Lifestyle*, etc.)

- *Architectural Digest*
  The leading consumer magazine on home decor.
  www.condenet.com/mags/archdigest

- *Fine Furnishings International Magazine*
  It includes a "great finds" product showcase.
  www.ffimagazine.com

- *Home Accents Today*
  A trade magazine with information about home accessories and retailers.
  www.homeaccentstoday.com

- *Home Furnishings News*
  Trade magazine about home products retailing.
  www.hfnmag.com

- *Interior Design Magazine*
  The website includes a searchable buyers guide.
  www.interiordesign.net

- *Metropolitan Home*
  Reports on trends and hot products.
  www.metropolitanhome.com

Jewelry

- *The Authority on Jewelry Manufacturing*
  A magazine devoted to the manufacture and sale of fine and fashion jewelry.
  www.ajm-magazine.com

- *Diamond Registry Bulletin Excerpts*
  A trade publication with information about new styles, popular designers and prices. Has a column on buying diamond jewelry.
  www.diamondregistry.com/News/index.htm

- *NationalJeweler.com*
  An online trade magazine with tips on top jewelery retailers and other industry news.
  www.nationaljeweler.com

Lifestyle Publications

If you work with wealthy clients, it's a good idea to read the consumer magazines they are reading so that you will become familiar with the types of products and services they expect. The following publications feature the finest products of all kinds – fashion, food, gifts, jewelry, and housewares, as well as features on travel.

- *Millionaire Magazine*
  www.millionaire.com

- *Robb Report*
  www.robbreport.com

- *Town & Country*
  www.townandcountrymag.com

Concierge Services

If you're considering offering concierge services, many of the publications above will be helpful. Also read local newspapers that list theatrical and musical performances and other one-time or short-run events, from car shows to spectator sports of all kinds. And keep abreast of local sports magazines for places to play various amateur sports and for professional sports competitions.

- *Concierge.com*
  Offers advice on vacation planning and includes information about *Conde Nast Traveler* magazine.
  www.concierge.com

7.3 Business Resources

Websites

- *SCORE*
  The Service Corps Of Retired Executives has volunteers throughout the U.S. who donate time to mentor small businesses free of charge. Their site has helpful articles.
  www.score.org

- *Small Business Administration*
  The SBA is an excellent resource with advice on business licenses and taxes as well as general information on starting a business.
  www.sbaonline.sba.gov

- *Online Small Business Workshop*
  The Canadian government offers an Online Small Business Workshop which includes information about taxes, financing, incorporation, and other topics.
  www.cbsc.org/osbw/workshop.cfm

- *Nolo.com Small Business Legal Encyclopedia*
  Nolo is a publisher of legal information presented in plain English. Their website also offers free advice on a variety of other small business matters.
  www.nolo.com

- *Seven Steps to Starting Your Own Business*
  StartUpBiz.com offers helpful step-by-step business advice plus links to many useful resources.
  http://www.startupbiz.com/7Steps/Seven.html

Organizations

- *American Purchasing Society*
  This organization publishes *Professional Purchasing*, and offers a variety of services as well as Certified Purchasing Professional (CPP) certification. Membership costs $188 for new members, and $129 in subsequent years.
  www.american-purchasing.com

- *National Federation of Independent Business*
  NFIB gives members access to many business products and services at discounted costs. Membership costs $200 per year.
  www.nfib.com

- *National Retail Federation*
  The world's largest retail organization with members from 50 countries. Members include May, Federated and The Gap. While this organization is only for retail companies and not individuals, the website is a valuable resource for news about what's happening in the retail business.
  www.nrf.com

More Fabulous Books

Find out how to break into the "fab" job of your dreams with FabJob career guides. Each 2-in-1 set includes a print book and CD-ROM.

Get Paid to Help People Look Fabulous

Imagine having an exciting high paying job showing people and companies how to make a fabulous impression. **FabJob Guide to Become an Image Consultant** shows you how to:

- Do image consultations and advise people about: total image makeovers, communication skills, wardrobe, and corporate image

- Start an image consulting business, price your services, and find clients

- Select strategic partners such as makeup artists, hair stylists, and cosmetic surgeons

- Have the polished look and personal style of a professional image consultant

Get Paid to Decorate

Imagine having a rewarding high paying job that lets you use your creativity to make homes and businesses beautiful and comfortable. **FabJob Guide to Become an Interior Decorator** shows you how to:

- Teach yourself interior decorating (includes step-by-step decorating instructions)

- Get 10-50% discounts on furniture and materials

- Create an impressive portfolio even if you have no previous paid decorating experience

- Get a job with a retailer, home builder or other interior design industry employer

- Start an interior decorating business, price your services, and find clients

Visit www.FabJob.com to order guides today!